Way Back in the Hills

Hills

Book 2

'Fesser Goes to
College

JAMES C.
HEFLEY

HANNIBAL
BOOKS
Hannibal, Missouri 63401

Dedicated to
CLARA STRONG KENT
who was more than a teacher to me.
She was also an encourager and friend.

Copyright James C. Hefley
FIRST PRINTING 1996
ISBN 0-929292-820
ALL RIGHTS RESERVED
Printed in the United States of America by Lithocolor
Press, Inc.
Cover design by Cyndi Allison

(Use coupon in back to order more of this and
other books from HANNIBAL BOOKS)

Behind the Scenes

Fesser Goes to College is a sequel to **Way Back in the Hills**, the story of my childhood in the Arkansas Ozarks. This second book, like the first, is a melding of recorded history, conversations with people of the era, memory and imagination.

The faculty and staff of the mid-forties are presented as real people. Most student characters are fictional creations and are not to be identified as actual persons attending Tech during that period.

Special thanks go to Alumni Director Sharon Mullens and the Tomlinson Library staff for assistance in research. Microfilmed copies of the *Arka-Tech* student newspaper and alumni and faculty profiles were especially helpful in documenting personalia and college events.

The best single source was Kenneth R. Walker's 935-page **History of Arkansas Tech University 1909-1992**, published by ATU in 1992. Dr. Walker is Professor of History at ATU and a masterful compiler of events, statistics and persons associated with Arkansas Tech history.

Special thanks must also be extended to Professor John Rollow and a select group of alumni who shared their Tech memories during interviews.

"To live in hearts we leave behind, is not to die," wrote the English poet Thomas Campbell. How true. How satisfying.

Hannibal, Missouri
January, 1996

Contents

Chapter 1

"Mama Wanted Me To Be a Doctor"

On a cool December evening, in 1933, my daddy
— Frederick Joseph Hefley — stomped into
our log cabin and swung me around and around
before the fireplace. "Wanna go huntin' with me
tonight?" he teased.

"Yeah, yeah," I squealed.

My dark-haired mama — Hester Hosanna Foster
Hefley — cuffed Daddy playfully on his forearm. "Fred,
he's only three years old. He cain't hunt with you yet.
Come on to the table before your supper gets cold."

Daddy wolfed down two tin cups of cornbread
and milk and a little slab of pork belly which Mama
had fried over the fireplace. Then he lit his lantern,
grabbed his .22 rifle and gave Mama a quick hug.
"I'm takin' ole Lion and ole Muse for a run up the
Old House Holler. Be back by midnight."

We were living then in a two room log-cabin that
had been built by one of Daddy's uncles before the
turn of the century. A pole loft hung from the ceiling

above my bed. Light streamed through a small box window to the left of the big fireplace. When darkness fell, Mama lit the "coal oil" kerosene lamp.

Mama cooked whatever she could scrounge from our storm cellar on a wood stove. When supplies ran low, she served corn bread and milk in tin cups. We just ate whatever was available and sometimes went to bed wanting more.

Daddy never knew from one day to the next when he would work for Roosevelt's WPA. He would saddle up our mare, Ole Babe, before dawn, ride five miles down the valley to see if the crew boss needed him. If we saw him coming up the trail before midday, we knew he had struck out. When he didn't get home for supper, we knew he had a day's wages coming.

Often all we had to eat was the game that Daddy killed. When he left with his dogs Mama, who had been a teacher before my birth, taught me the basics in made-up verse, one of her ways of preparing me for school.

> A is for apple,
> B is for ball.
> C stands for coon dogs,
> Ole Lion, Muse, and all....

When we finished the alphabet, she stuck a chicken feather in my hair and drilled me on numbers as we danced in the light of the lamp and fireplace.

> One little, two little, three little Indians,
> Four little, five little, six little Indians,
> Seven little, eight little, nine little Indians.
> Ten little Indian boys!

The song was really quite appropriate since Mama had Cherokee blood.

Mama gave me a good head start on my education. By the time I was three I could recite the alphabet forwards and backwards and could count to 100. I could also spell two big jaw breakers, MEDITERRANEAN and CZECHOSLOVAKIA, which Mama never tired of having me spout before company. Then after my showoff, she'd announce, "James Carl is going to college one day and study to be a doctor. Just like his great-grandpa Simon Solomon Sutton on the Other Creek."

If you read my book, *Way Back in the Hills*, you know that our log cabin was tucked into a mountain cove, five miles up Big Creek Valley from Mt. Judea, in Newton County, Arkansas.

"Foreigners" pronounced our nearest town the way it appeared on the state map, "Mount Judea." To me the little berg where Daddy sold his possum, coon, fox, and mink hides was just "Judy."

Big Creek, which runs near Judy, is a tributary of the wild Buffalo River. Big Creek forks three miles up from where it pours into the Buffalo, splitting the rugged terrain into two deep valleys. When someone on either fork said, "I'm goin' over on the Other Creek," folks knew exactly what they meant.

Though we had neither electricity, plumbing nor telephones, I never felt deprived. How could I be with a flock of cousins, loving parents, grandparents, aunts and uncles living all around?

The weekly *Kansas City Star* and the *Newton County Informer* were delivered by Uncle John Holt on horseback to the wooden mailbox that was nailed to the side of a white oak tree down the hill from our cabin.

The papers gave us a window to the outside world of the mid 1930s. We read about baseball, President Roosevelt's New Deal, and the growing power of the German spell binder, Adolph Hitler. Such news seemed far from our peaceful valley and the concerns of our extended families.

Grandpa and Grandma Hefley lived a half mile below us, near the creek, in the oldest house in the valley. Most of their 11 children farmed within a mile of the home place. Mama's people lived along the sides of the Other Creek Valley, a good day's walk from our cabin.

Mama's maternal grandfather had been the famous Doctor Simon Solomon Sutton, who rode a yellow mare on sick calls. Two of his sons went away to college and became lawyers. One, Taylor Sutton, ran for lieutenant governor of Arkansas, but lost. Mama was always bragging about her doctor granddaddy and her lawyer uncles.

Doctoring was Mama's first choice for me. "If not a doctor, then a lawyer," she would say. "Lawyers become governors and senators. Either way, you'll need to study hard and go on to college."

Like most folks back in the hills, Mama's daddy, Grandpa Pulliam Foster, and my father's family, didn't place much stock in education. Grandma Barbara Jane Sutton Foster didn't encourage me either. She'd suffered from poor eyesight all her life. "No doctor was ever able to help me," she lamented. "Not even my daddy."

Only my mama seemed to have a vision of what an education could mean. She was the only one of the six Foster children to attend high school. To do that she boarded with her Uncle John Sutton and attended the North Arkansas Baptist Academy, in the western part of Newton County, near the hamlet of Parthenon. Mama was ready for the 11th grade when the school had to close due to a cutoff of funds. If Mama had finished high school, she could have gone to Arkansas Tech, 65 miles south of Judy in the big town of Russellville. Everybody in Big Creek Valley knew about Tech and its all-star football team which had played West Point in 1923. Two valley boys, G.W. and Elmer Hamm, had been on that squad with the legendary John Tucker.

Mama still managed to get her teacher's license. Then, while living with her parents, she walked ten miles round trip to teach eight grades at the one-room Macedonia School on Kent Mountain between the two valleys.

She met Daddy at a community picnic, held at Lurton, some 15 miles south of Macedonia, on Arkansas Hwy 7. She was 20 and he only 16, but he must have taken quite a shine to her. He always said, "She was the purtiest girl in the county."

Mama held aspirations beyond teaching in a one-room mountain grade school. Becoming a woman doctor or lawyer was now out of the question. Cousin Eva, who lived in Springfield, Missouri, came down for a visit and told Mama about Draughon's Business College. "You could live with me and my husband," she said. Mama took her teaching savings and struck out for Springfield.

Worried that Mama might be courted by some

fancy Dan in the big city, Daddy came to be near her. Mama paid his tuition and he roomed with his cousin Lowell Hefley. When Mama's money ran out, she and Daddy came back to Arkansas where they were married by a Justice of the Peace under a big whiteoak tree near the south fork of Big Creek. The date was July 28, 1928. Mama was 21 and Daddy 17.

Mama got a job teaching school at Red Rock in the Other Creek Valley and she and Daddy lived in the back of the school. When I was born in 1930, she quit to spend full time with her baby. "Fred," she told Daddy, "you'll have to make our living." Daddy farmed, hunted, trapped, and worked on Roosevelt's WPA, building roads for $1.20 a day.

I had Mama to myself for three-and-a-half years. Then my brother Howard Jean arrived on Christmas Day, 1933. Not long after that our mare, Ole Babe, produced a colt we named Timbrook. I didn't know where either came from, but all in all the colt was much more impressive.

Mama was "in the family way" again when Grandma Eller Hefley died. My paternal grandmother had borne 14 children. A set of triplets had died at birth, but she lived to see the other eleven grown before suffering a fatal heart attack at 57.

Grandma Foster came from across the mountain to visit us and help Mama when her time grew near. "Grandma," I asked, "why is Mama's belly so big?" Grandma brushed me off. Daddy took me and Howard Jean down to Grandpa Tom Hefley's to spend the night. My Uncle Loma and Aunt Clara Hefley were living with him since Grandma Eller had died.

About mid-morning the next day, Daddy came rushing down to Grampa Tom's house. "Lomy, go git Doc Sexton. Hester's time has come."

Time for what? I didn't know what Daddy meant. About two hours later I heard a car put-putting up the creek road. When the car came in sight, I screeched, "Doc Sexton!" I was all excited and jumping up and down. After all Doc had the only car in Big Creek Valley, and I didn't get to see it often.

The car jolted to a stop at the end of the lane below Grandpa Tom's house. Doc, a peppery, stocky redhead, came striding up to the house just in time to meet Daddy coming back from our cabin.

Doc and I met Daddy in Grampa's peach orchard. "Son, you stay here," Daddy ordered. I watched them disappear up the trail to our cabin.

Doc came back without Daddy a few hours later. He held up two fingers and grinned with satisfaction. "Hester and her twin girls are doin' just fine."

"What twin girls?" I asked.

Doc grinned. "You'll see them when you go home. One on each side of your mama."

Not long after Louise and Loucille were born, Mama enrolled me in the Holt-Hamilton School. The one-room building was perched near Big Creek, four miles up the valley from our cabin. Teacher Valera Copeland had been one of Mama's grade school classmates.

One Friday Miss Copeland came home with me to spend the night. She bragged to Mama that I was way ahead of the others in the first grade, and that she was moving me up to the second grade. Mama sat by the fireplace beaming. "Good, good. He's going to college one day and make something of himself. I'm hopin' he'll be a doctor."

Saturday morning, while Miss Copeland was still visiting with Mama, Daddy left to cut firewood. Tired of hearing woman talk, I slipped outside to catch blue-bellied lizards on the back yard fence. I was creeping toward a big, fat one when the back door squeaked open. Mama popped out

"James Carl, your daddy's cuttin' firewood up by the graveyard," Mama said. "Go take him his dinner and a jug of water. Take ole Lion with you."

Daddy was chopping on a log near the little cemetery where my Grandma Eller Hefley, Great-grandpa Jim Hefley, Great-uncle Albert Hefley, and Cousin Dennis Holt lay buried.

Daddy grabbed the jug from my grubby hands. Gulp, gulp, gulp. He drank half before putting the jug down. "Pshaw, boy. That was real good. You should uf come two 'airs ago."

"Yoh, yoh! Yoh, yoh, yoh." Ole Lion jumped a cottontail, chasing it into the graveyard and underneath the little house that had been built over Cousin Dennis' final resting place. The dog began pawing at the dirt to get in the house.

"Daddy," I squealed. "He'll dig up Cousin Dennis!"

Daddy ran into the burying ground, and grabbed Lion by the collar. The rabbit skittered from under the grave house and into a blackberry thicket.

Daddy saw the fright in my eyes. "Son, Dennis is six foot under. Ain't no dawg gonna dig up his bones."

I hung outside the graveyard fence while Daddy

smoothed the ground where the dog had dug.

Daddy slipped over and put a reassuring arm on my shoulder. "Son, there ain't nuthin' in that graveyard for you to be scared uf."

"Yes, but Uncle Willie Pink says…" Daddy knew I was thinking of his older brother's scary graveyard tales. Every time he and Aunt Blanche came down the mountain to stay the night, I spent two hours shivering under the covers in fright.

"Pay no 'taintion to yer ole uncle," Daddy advised. "I'm gonna have a talk with 'em about scarin' kids. Now you'd better skitter on home."

Mama had my tin dinner plate filled with corn bread and molasses when I arrived. After supper she tucked the twins in their dresser drawer beds and led Brother to the bed where he and I slept. She then sat down beside me on my bench at the kitchen table and stroked my black hair. "You're a good boy, James Carl," she purred. "You came straight home."

"Yessum, and the reason," I admitted, "is that I didn't want to stay around the graveyard whar' Daddy was eatin' his dinner."

Mama flashed me a look that said we'd discussed this before. She wasn't surprised at my question: "How old was Dennis when he died?"

"Almost 11. About the same age as your daddy was then, I think. I was a teenager and heard about Dennis from my Grampa Sutton. He was one of the doctors that tried to save the boy. Doc Sexton sent word for him to come."

"What kilt Dennis? Nobody ever tolt me."

"Dennis fell out of a tree and broke his leg. After

the doctors put it back in place, he got blood poisoned. They sawed his leg off above the knee, but didn't get all the poison. It must have gone to his heart."

Mama eyed me curiously. "Why do you want to know all this? You're too little to be worryin' about things that happened long ago."

"Mama, Uncle Willie Pink says people of all ages get sick and die. He tolt me and Cousin Glen once, 'If you boys don't believe that, cut a twine string as long as you're tall. Take it to the graveyard and ya'll find yer size.' That's what Uncle Willie Pink said."

Mama's eyes flashed. "Yer Uncle Pink just likes to scare little kids. He's just funnin'. He don't mean no harm."

"But Mama, little kids do die, don't they?"

"Yes, she admitted. "But if you study to be a doctor, you can help keep some little ones from dying too soon." Then she bent down and gave me a reassuring hug.

December came again. Daddy took his fur hides to Judy and brought back a bucket of lard, a box of Arm & Hammer baking soda, a sack of flour, a little poke of salt and a few other necessities.

The Hamilton-Holt School had closed and I transferred to the White House School.

Christmas Eve fell on a Thursday in 1936. We trooped down the creek to the White House School for a big party. Like most Big Creek families, we didn't do much decorating at home. The gathering at the school was the big event of the season. On Christmas morning we got an orange apiece and perhaps a penny stick of candy.

The day after Christmas, Daddy saddled Ole Babe. He swept Mama up into the saddle, then handed Loucille to her. With Brother and I skipping along ahead of Ole Babe, Daddy carried the other twin, Louise, and led the way. We were going over the mountain to see Mama's family.

Two miles and four creek fords down the valley, we turned north up the mountain. Passing through a big gap in the bluff, we followed a narrow trail alongside Grampa Foster's corn field to the cabin where Mama had lived as a girl. Grampa met us before we got there. We had to shout to pierce his deafness. Grandma came shuffling out of the house, arms extended, peering through her dim eyes, trying to make out our faces.

When the sun came out the next morning we walked a mile down the Red Rock side of the mountain to visit Mama's Uncle John Sutton and his family. "They're stayin' on my grandparents' old place now," Mama explained.

After dinner Mama led me down the hill to a grove of green cedars and pointed to two tombstones. I read the names, Simon Solomon and Mary Ann Sutton. "Your great-grandparents," Mama said proudly. "Grandma Sutton died first. Grandpa, the doctor, passed on the year after you were born."

"What'd he die from, Mama?" I asked.

"He was goin' to a doctors' meeting. Stepped off the train in Little Rock and slipped on a banana peelin'. Fell and broke his leg. Came home on crutches and never got any better."

Mama's eyes watered up. "All my grampa ever wanted to do was help sick people get well, and he couldn't help hisself."

We had just returned from our visit with Mama's kinfolks when Grampa Tom Hefley keeled over from a stroke while attending a singing school at Judy. "Take him home and put him to bed," Doc Sexton said. "There ain't nuthin' we can do for him."

Grandma Eller Hefley had been dead for three years. Now a sad-faced, lonesome Grampa lay in bed trying to talk.

"Can't Doc Sexton cure Grandpa?" I asked Mama.

Mama shook her head sadly. "Maybe some day doctors will be able to help stroke victims."

Though I was only seven, Daddy let me help him with the corn harvest. We were too poor to own a farm wagon. Ole Babe pulled a sled beside the corn rows. I trooped along beside Daddy, pitching ears that mostly missed the sled. Daddy always wanted me to feel that I was a big help.

Great-grandpa Jim Hefley, Grandpa Tom and my daddy had all attended the one room White House school which probably got its name because it was the first building in the valley painted white. It was probably the first building to be painted.

Teacher Clara Strong Kent, a spunky redhead read to us from the Bible every morning before classes. She and two of her sisters had attended the Baptist Academy at Parthenon ahead of Mama. Their farmer daddy, John, decreed that all four of his daughters would go to college. Neighbors laughed; "when all they'll do is come home and get married."

John wasn't deterred. "If they cain't take care of me when ah'm old, maybe they'll have enough pull to git me in the poor house." His four daughters all became teachers.

Clara — it was the custom in the hills for children to call adults by their first names — was all business at the White House. After the morning Bible reading, she divided her students into learning groups, and had one bunch at a time come to the front and recite.

Mama's home schooling put me at the head of my class. Clara made me an "assistant teacher" to drill the first and second grades in their lessons. "You kids pay attention to James Carl," she ordered.

Friday afternoons, Clara divided us into teams for the weekly ciphering and spelling matches. She began with simple math — "how much is six plus six?" — and ended with seventh and eighth graders doing cube roots and equations. One by one, she tossed problems at us until only the winner remained standing. I usually won.

For spelling, she had two captains choose sides. She tossed words from one side to the other.

"Charlene, spell incontrovertible."

"I n c o n t r o v e r t a b l e."

"Wrong. Jenny, on Joe's team, how do you spell it."

"I n c o n t r o v e r t i b l e."

"Correct. Score one for Joe's team."

Back and forth, Clara pitched the words until one team had won.

When Clara urged us to start thinking about high school and college, invariably, someone would say, "But Miss Kent, it's too far for me to walk to the high school at Judy."

"Yes, it is," Clara agreed. "I understand. But if there is any way you can, you need to continue your education. Before you even finish high school, be thinking of college and what you'd like to do with your life. You might become a doctor, a lawyer, a scientist or a teacher like me."

At this point I always raised my hand. "Mama wants me to be a doctor. Like my great-grandpa Sutton was on the Other Creek. Like Doc Walter Sexton is here now on Big Creek."

"You'll have to attend college and then medical school," Clara explained. Her eyes swept the room. "But James Carl, if you or anyone else on this creek really wants to be somebody, you'll have to finish high school and go to college."

Clara and Mama were of one mind on that. Never mind that I wasn't even ten yet. "Get your high school diploma at Judy and go on to Arkansas Tech in Russellville." Clara said. "That's where I study in the summer. Tech isn't far away and it's only a junior college. You can go two years there and then transfer to the university in Fayetteville."

I tucked that away in my little brain, thinking, *That's what I'll do.*

Chapter 2

"A Four-year Goof-off"

My three years at the White House passed quickly. There were two three-month terms a year. By taking a grade each term I was ready for high school in 1939. Counting my baby sister, Jimmie Fern, Mama now had five young'uns to look after, but she still helped me with my lessons whenever possible.

Another addition to our family provided entertaining diversion. A mail-order Silvertone radio and battery. Each evening I could tune in to hear Jack Armstrong, Captain Midnight and other spine-tingling adventure serials. On Saturday nights the dial was turned to 650, WSM Nashville, and the whole family gathered around to listen to the Grand Ole Opry.

My world view was enlarged by listening to the news programs. War darkened the radio waves. Radio commentator Walter Winchell rattled off the somber news, night after night:

Good evening, Mr. and Mrs. North America and all the ships at sea. The war is spreading

across Europe. Britain is conscripting men for its
army and Mr. Churchill, the new British prime
minister, is warning Hitler that time is running out
on peace.

At our house, talk of moving was in the air. I was
a month short of nine years old when Daddy rode our
mare to Judy and caught a ride in a truck to the county
seat at Jasper. He woke us all up when he got home
around midnight, announcing that he had sold our 61
acres to Uncle Sam's Forest Service for $264. I heard
him tell Mama, "I'm buying us 40 acres and a house
and barn for $240, a mile out Highway 123 from
Judy."

Mama hugged me tight. "We're moving closer to
Judy so you can attend high school. You'll start in
August. Soon you'll be ready for college."

The following Saturday Daddy and Uncle Loma
packed all our worldly goods into Grampa Tom's
wagon. Grampa told us goodbye from his bed. Mama
explained once more that we were moving so I could
go to high school and one day become a doctor.
Grampa's stroke had tied his tongue and he couldn't
reply. "I just hope he understands," Mama sighed.

Mama and baby Jimmie rode old Babe. The twins
sat on a straw mattress in the wagon bed. Brother and
I climbed up on the spring seat beside Daddy and
Uncle Loma, who would bring the wagon back to
Grampa's.

"Hi, ya, giddy up," Daddy cracked. We were off.

Three hours later we pulled into the yard of the
unpainted frame house. My brother, nicknamed
Monk, and I scampered inside to look it over. We
discovered there were four rooms and a back porch

with a big concrete cistern that caught rain water as it came off the roof. It was about fifty feet to the barn which set next to a pond, and a half mile to the spring where we got our drinking water.

There was no plumbing or electricity, but we felt as if we had really moved up-town. Judy was only a mile away with a population of 50 or 60. That seemed like a lot of people to us, even though most of them were related to us.

Come August, Mama took me to Judy to sign up for the ninth grade. "He finished at the White House," Mama reported to "Uncle" Guy Hefley (Daddy's first cousin), the towering superintendent. "Clara Kent says he's ready for the ninth grade. He took two grades a year at the White House."

Uncle Guy excused himself to confer with two teachers and then came back to Mama. "He looks way too little for high school. We're going to enter him in the eighth grade and see how he does."

Mama protested that I'd be taking the eighth grade twice. Uncle Guy stood his ground. Mama sighed, "Well, son, I guess you'll just have to do the eighth grade over. We're not gonna change his mind."

That afternoon I shuffled down the road to Leck Greenhaw's house. He saw me coming and came out on the porch. "Howdy, neighbor. Whut's on yer mind today?"

"I've been listening to the war news on KWTO from Springfield."

He talked to me as if I were grown. "Do you think England is going to declare war on Germany?"

"Walter Winchell," I replied, "says ole Churchill will go to war if Germany invades another country. Hitler has already gobbled up Austria and Czechoslovakia. Winchell thinks Poland could be next."

For the next half hour we batted war views back and forth until Leck said, "Well, I've gotta slop the hogs and feed the cows. Come over ag'in and we'll talk more world news."

My eighth grade teacher, Herbert Edwards, lived just across the road from Leck. I was his star pupil. I could do math problems faster than anybody, and if Herbert had a spare minute, I'd query him about the war news.

Mama had another baby, sister Freddie, the following January, but the real excitement began when a crew of men began putting up big tar-soaked poles across our pasture and stringing wire that would bring electricity to the valley. The wires ran up to Judy and beyond as the rural electrification project brought our county into the 20th century. No longer would be have to worry about the radio batteries wearing out so we'd miss our favorite programs until we could save up enough money to replace them. We even got electric lights.

As if six kids and a garden weren't enough to keep my mother busy, she opened a store in the room where the twins slept. She started by buying six boxes of Arm & Hammer Baking Soda for a quarter and selling them for a nickel a box. Soon she had a whole shelf of groceries to sell. "I didn't go to business college for nothin'," she informed us.

24

In 1941, my second year in high school, Mama and Daddy bought the vacant Roy Milum corner store in Judy. Doc Sexton's office sat between our store and Cousin Lloyd Hefley's store, which also housed the U. S. Post Office. Farther up the street, you could buy a hamburger for a dime at Nichols' cafe. If you needed your horse shoed, Uncle Willie Pink Hefley was the man to see at the blacksmith shop on the east end of Judy town.

Mama stuck to the store. Daddy majored in the dog business. He bought bluetick pups, trained them to hunt coons, then placed ads in hunting magazines, offering the young dogs for sale to out-of-staters.

December 7, 1941 — "a day that will live in infamy," Franklin Delano Roosevelt declared. America was at war against Japan, Germany and Italy. People without radios poured into Judy to hear the latest news.

Kinfolk began leaving for the west coast to work in defense plants, some never to return. The Newton County Draft Board began tapping men for service. Daddy, with six children, was ordered to report to Little Rock for a pre-induction physical. The doctors found a hernia and sent him back to us.

While the war raged, school continued at the WPA-built stone high school on the hill in back of Judy. About 90 high schoolers lounged behind old-fashioned desks in one big room. Freshmen sat on the left side near the big pot-bellied stove, and almost roasted in winter. Sophomores occupied the next rows, then juniors, with seniors so far from the stove that they became chilled during the cold season.

Some boys dropped out for military service. Clara Kent's cousin Wilson Strong volunteered for the Marines. He would die on Iwo Jima. Calvin Hill, a member of my class, and Bailey Greenhaw, a neighbor to us would also make the ultimate sacrifice for their country.

My best chum, David Criner, and I were in no danger of being drafted. David limped badly, the aftermath of a bout with polio. I was far too young.

My four years at Mt. Judea High School amounted to one long vacation from serious scholastics. I didn't have Clara to egg me on. Mama had her hands full waiting on customers and kids, although on occasions she asked about my school subjects. Daddy was occupied with his coon dogs. Spring, summer, and fall, I fished for bass. During the winter I played checkers and a card game called "pitch" and went on buying trips with Daddy. School was more of an afterthought.

Late summer was watermelon buying time. My brother Monk and I piled into our Model A truck cab with Daddy and a hound dog. We headed south, where I got my first look at the Arkansas Tech campus on the northern fringe of Russellville. While we were there we saw Naval Air Cadets marching on the football field. "This is where I'm going to college," I told Monk. "Mama wants me to study to be a doctor." Monk wasn't impressed.

Daddy turned north toward Mount Nebo and stopped at a house partway up the slope. The farmer hailed us joyfully, "Howdy, boys. Ah've got some of the sweetest melons you'uns evah tasted. Hep yerselves."

He split a big ripe melon open. Monk and I dived in. Yum, yum. The juice coursed down our necks, dribbling under our overalls, leaking on the ground. With Daddy's help, we finished off two big ones. We got so full that the farmer and his sons had to load up the truck. Daddy paid for the melons and we headed back. Passing between Tech's big, white-columned administration building and the football field, I threw up through the open truck window.

When I didn't have anything better to do in Judy, I slouched on our store porch, listening to the old men argue the Bible. Next to the Saturday night movie held in a tent pitched beside Nichols' Cafe, arguing the Bible was the most entertaining spectator sport in Judy.

Mama kept asking if I didn't need to study my lessons. "A boy headed for college, oughta be at the head of his class," she said.

"Don't worry, Mama, I'll be ready for Tech when the time comes." That was my standard answer.

During four years of high school, I never took a book home to study. Still, I made a B average. The only way you could fail then at Judy High School was to drop out. I'm not blaming my teachers. I just preferred fishing and playing games to studying.

More than anyone else, David Criner kept my brain from atrophying. Shy and timid around girls, he came alive when I asked him a question about the war, politics, history, big league baseball, literature, anything. Fishing buddies, we spent hours hanging off a creek bluff, talking about anything and everything that crossed our minds.

One Saturday morning, David and I were lounging on the front porch of Nichols' Cafe, arguing about American strategy in the Pacific. Jeames Nichols, who was married to one of my older first cousins, sat nearby, stroking a hound dog's ear. "Boys," he interrupted, "do you understand all them big words yer pitchin' around?"

I puffed out my scrawny chest. "Oh, shore."

David pulled a paperback dictionary from his pocket and handed it to Jeames. "Ask us some definitions."

"I've got a better idee," Jeames said. "David, you take the dictionary and ask James Carl whut a word means. Then, James Carl, you ax him one. See who can set the otter 'un down the quickest."

So the contest went. An 11 and a 15-year-old throwing jawbreakers at each other while the crowd kept growing around us. I've forgotten who won. I just remember Jeames saying to me, "Son, yer a regular little 'fesser." The monicker stuck.

My mischievous, burr-headed little brother, Howard Jean, had gotten his nickname for a different skill. Uncle Lloyd was out hunting with some of us and saw Howard Jean scramble up a tall white oak to punch a squirrel out of a hole. "That boy's a real possum," Uncle Lloyd declared.

"More lack a monkey," someone else said.

"Monkey" stuck and was shortened to Monk.

Most days, instead of going to school, Monk headed for the creek or woods. While I didn't bother to bring books home, during four years of high school I missed only two days because of measles.

Mama was still counting on me going to college to prepare for medical school. She kept talking about her Grandpa Sutton and Doc Sexton, who saw patients in his office just a few feet from our store.

Then Doc Sexton disappointed everybody by moving 55 miles south to Dover — I never knew why.

A new doc moved into Doc Sexton's old office. Aged and almost blind, Doc Simpson (not his real name) spent most of his time on our store porch with other hangers-on.

Cousin Gussie Nichols, Jeames's wife, got in the family way. The baby started coming sooner than expected. Jeames raced down the street for Doc Simpson. Roused out of bed, the old medic grabbed a pair of pants and ran to Gussie's bedside. In the confusion, Doc forgot to tie the umbilical cord. Jeames and Gussie's baby bled to death.

Mama came away shaking her head. "That baby would have lived if we'd had a decent doctor." Mama didn't say it, but I knew she was thinking that I should become that doctor.

I began the 12th grade in August, 1943. Allied planes were pounding German and Italian cities. The Red Army had the German army on the run in eastern Europe. Mussolini's Italian Fascist government had fallen from power. Americans were regaining strategic island bases in the Pacific.

The war had put more money into the economy. Gas rationing forced the few people who owned automobiles to stay home and spend more money in Judy. When Mama saw me sitting by the stove whittling, she said, "You need something more worthwhile to do.

"I'll order a dozen dollar watches," she proposed. "For each one you sell after school, you'll make a quarter. When you sell them all, we'll pay the watch company and you can keep your profit."

I earned three big greenback dollars. "Isn't that better than whittlin'?" Mama asked. I nodded.

A month or so later, Mama showed me a candy punchboard that had come in the mail. "The customers pay a dime a punch," she explained. "The winning numbers get a big ole pecan log candy bar. And we make $4 profit on every board. Now," she said, "how would you like to be the punchboard man and make that profit on top of your watch money?"

My eyes bulged. "Yeah, Mama."

I earned four more big dollars. When that board was punched out, Mama ordered another one for me. During the next two months I made enough money to order a bicycle from Sears & Roebuck. Riding my bike sure beat walking to the creek to go fishing.

Mama was smart. My business ventures kept me in the store where I could help her with other sales. Otherwise, she knew I'd just be killing time on the creek bank or loafing around Judy.

Mama hadn't forgotten our reason for moving to Judy. "You don't need to know much to run a little country store," she said. "You'll need a college education to really make something of yourself."

High school graduation was only a few months

away, and Mama was trying to revive my flagging interest in college. Daddy didn't seem to care. None of his ten brothers and sisters had studied beyond high school, and I guess he figured they were making out all right.

Daddy now had 11 coonhounds in his pen across the street. My brother, Monk, had given a farmer two dollars for a yellow mongrel pup he called "Danny Boy." With part of my money earned from merchandising, I bought a brown shepherd pup. Naturally, I called him "Ole Shep."

The Judy school year began in August and ended in early March, in time for farm kids to help in planting. By January three of my seven classmates had already made college plans. C.B. Hudson and Junior Johnson were planning to enter Tech for the spring term which began in March, 1944. Billie Nichols was planning on starting in September. The other four hadn't made up their minds yet. That left me, at 13, the youngest member of the class.

"I'm sending off to Tech for a catalog and enrollment information," Mama informed me.

I rolled my eyes, but said only, "Yes, Mama."

March came too soon. I brought home my final grade card from Judy school for Mama and Daddy to sign. I had Bs in Psychology, English, Democracy, and Conservation. For Business Arithmatic, teacher-principal Wilburn McCutcheon gave me an A.

Mama looked my final Judy grade card over good. Then she pulled out a big envelope she had received from Arkansas Tech.

She showed me the college catalog that contained

a listing of the faculty and the courses offered. The thought of leaving Judy and being on my own with a couple of classmates gave me an adrenaline rush.

"I'm going to college Mama. This month. C.B. and Junior are already signed up."

"Well, you could stay here and help me in the store full time," Mama said. "At 13 you're too young to work in a sawmill."

"Nah, I want to go to Tech. I'm smart enough."

"Well, I expect you are, but yer just so young. You'll have to take mostly required courses the first year. Then you can decide on a major."

Mama raised her apron to wipe her eyes. In her heart of hearts, I knew she'd rather I stay home. What was best for her children came first with Mama. It always had.

Mama, who handled all the business affairs in our family, helped me fill out the application. She slipped the paper into an envelope with my senior report card from Mt. Judy High School and said, "Take it to the post pffice."

Suddenly I thought of something. "Mama, whar will I be stayin'?"

"Oh, I've talked with my cousin Jane Essex in Russellville. She said you could stay with her and her husband, George. You'll eat breakfast and supper there and eat dinner at the college."

"I'll walk to Tech? How far is it?"

"Oh, no more than a mile. You can take your bike and ride it to class."

When I got back from the post office, Mama was telling Daddy what she had done. "James Carl's going to Tech," she announced.

Daddy didn't raise any objection. "Shore nuff? When's he goin'?" Daddy, four years younger than Mama, always let Mama make the big decisions in our family.

"The new term starts next week," Mama said, "If he doesn't go then, he'll have to wait another three months."

Daddy looked across at me and grinned. "When you come home, we'll go fishing."

I thumbed through the catalog, reading the unfamiliar names and boning up on the requirements. I looked across the store at Mama. "Says here, Mama, that Composition and Rhetoric is required. Does that have anything to do with grammar? I ain't very good with grammar."

"It includes grammar," Mama said. "The teacher will help you."

My high school graduation exercises came the next night. The four girls — Lois Hill (Calvin's sister), Billie Nichols, Dale McCutcheon, and Jewell Greenhaw — sat in hickory-bottom chairs on one side of the stage; we four boys — C.B. Hudson, Junior (Allen) Johnson, David Criner, and I — sat on the other side. Mama had stacked two pillows on my chair — "so everybody can see you." I perched there proudly in the first suit I'd ever worn, a $8.98 brown tweed which Mama had ordered from the Sears & Roebuck catalog.

The commencement address was given. Each of us walked briskly forward and received our diploma from Uncle Bill Hefley, chairman of the school board. The lean and lanky red-headed principal, Wilburn McCutcheon, noted that four of us had plans for college. "Four out of eight from a little school like Judy is pretty good," he said.

Wilburn thanked everybody for coming. Another of my uncles gave the benediction. I stepped down to shake Daddy's hand and receive a warm hug from Mama. It all seemed rather like a game to me, but to my teary-eyed mother it was deadly serious. "This," she said confidently, "is only the start for you, James Carl."

The die was cast. I, James Carl "'Fesser" Hefley was going to college.

Chapter 3

"Bound for Tech"

On the big day, Mama came to wake me before daylight. I was sleeping in my shirt tail, upstairs in the old Wes Berry Hotel, across the street from the store. Mama and Daddy had bought the seven-room, two-story building for $3,500.

"James Carl, do you know what day this is?" she teased.

"It's a good day to sleep."

"Guess again."

I was excited, but played along with Mama.

"This is the day you're going to college. Remember? We're taking you to Arkansas Tech. Get your britches on and wash your face and hands. Your daddy and the twins are already eatin' breakfast." Mama turned and walked back down the stairs.

The date was Monday, March 6, 1944. Three days after my high school graduation. Nine months past my 13th birthday. The world was still enmeshed in the most horrific war in history.

I rolled out of bed, pulled on my overalls and bounced barefoot down the stairs to the kitchen.

Daddy was wolfing down a big, fluffy biscuit, with molasses dripping down his chin. Louise, my eight-year-old twin sister, was squalling, "I wanna go to Russellville with James Carl. I wanna see Arkansas Tech." Loucille, the other twin, joined in. The younger girls, golden-haired, four-year-old Jimmie Fern, and curly-haired, three-year-old Freddie, were still sleeping.

Brother Monk came bounding into the room, his cur dog Danny Boy trailing after him. "Junior Nichols and me air goin' fishin' at the Rock Hole. Wanna come, 'Fesser?"

I already had my hands in the wash pan and didn't look up.

Mama was taking a broom to Danny Boy. "Out! Out!" She pushed Danny Boy through the back door and onto the porch. My dog, Shep, ducked into the kitchen. I shoved him back through the door and onto the porch before Mama could swat his behind.

Monk repeated his invitation. I tossed my little brother a superior smirk. "Don't you remember? I'm goin' to Russellville. I'm goin' to college. Ain't that right, Mama?"

Mama nodded proudly. "James Carl may be a doctor or a big businessman one day." She looked hard at Monk. "And you, young man had better be thinking of your education if you ever want to amount to anything."

Monk wasn't persuaded. He was ten years old and still in the second grade because he spent more time on the creek bank and in the woods than in the school house. He tried to divert Mama's attention to me. "'Fesser ain't cut out to be an ole doctor air some other big shot." He rolled his eyes in my direction. "Ah bet ya won't last a week at that ole Tech. You'll be wantin' to come home and go fishin'."

"I can come home for visits."

"Ya gonna take ole Shep with ya?" Monk asked.

Mama answered for me. "Shep's stayin' here. We'll take good care of him."

A wail resounded from the bedroom in back of the kitchen. Freddie. She woke Jimmie. Talk of college was put aside while Mama got my little sisters to the table. Daddy slipped out to feed his 11 bluetick coon hounds in the pen beside the house.

The living room door squeaked. "I've told your daddy a hundred times to oil that door," Mama grumbled.

It was only Uncle Arthur. "Hester, kin ya open the store fer me and mah buddies? We're goin' squirrel huntin' and need some loaf bread and baloney fer sandwiches."

"Mama," I moaned. "Tell them to get Uncle Lloyd to open his store. We'll never get started to Tech."

Mama shook her head. "Son, we're gonna be out of the store all day. We need the business."

Mama was thinking of her six kids and my college expenses. She sent me to the store with Uncle Arthur and his friends. I sold them what they wanted, closed the store and ran back across the street. Daddy had finished feeding his coonhounds and was now eager to get started to Russellville. I'd packed my college clothes in a cardboard box the night before.

Mama took the twins over to Cousin Gussie's.

Monk had already gone to the creek by the time she got back. Daddy cranked his Model A pickup and backed out of the garage. He tossed my suitcase and my bicycle in the back, then the five of us — Mama and Daddy, little Jimmie and Freddie, and me — loaded into the cab.

Mama happened to glance down and see my bare feet. Going barefooted was so natural I hadn't thought anything about it.

"James Carl," she commanded. "March right back upstairs and put on your shoes."

I raced back into the house. Just as I was getting back in the Model A, a flat-bed ton-and-a-half truck came roaring around the corner. Lum Hudson, the county judge, was taking his son, C.B. and his nephew, Junior Johnson to Tech.

Uncle Willie Pink came trotting down from his blacksmith shop, the gravy-spotted necktie that he always wore flopping in the wind.

It didn't matter to Uncle "P" that we were ready to leave. He didn't even ask where we were going. "Kin ya git me a twist of chawin' ta'baccer from the store 'fore ya leave town?"

Daddy cut the motor. "I'll go git P's 'baccer. The rest of you stay in the truck." Mama tapped his arm impatiently. "Hurry right back, Fred. We need to get on the road."

Ole Shep came trotting up. Before Mama could catch me, I was out of the truck and patting Shep's head. "I'll come home and see ya, ole feller. Ya be a good dog and do what Mama and Daddy tells ya. I'll be back and we'll go fishin' together."

Mama became impatient when she saw Uncle Pink come out of the store alone. "Son, go after your daddy."

I went running across the street, Ole Shep cavorting behind. Daddy was in the feed room taking money for a sack of seed corn from Burr McCutcheon, a coon hunting buddy, who had come in the back door of the store. "Daddy, hurry up," I piped. "I'll never get to Tech."

Ole Burr was spinning a yarn. Daddy, all ears, stood listening as if he had forgotten everything else. The front door dinged. Mama. "Fred, come on. Now!"

"I'm a'comin', Hester," Daddy promised. "Soon as ma buddy, hyar, finishes his story."

Mama stomped around the store, complaining until Burr shut up. "Now we're goin'," Mama declared. She marched across the street to the truck. Daddy cranked the engine again and jumped in. We pulled out of town with Shep barking and chasing us.

Put-putting south on Hwy 123, we climbed around horseshoe curves to the top of the mountain. Fifteen miles south of Judy, we rolled onto Hwy 7 and stopped for soda pop at Irving and Ruby Suttons' store in Lurton. "When you come home for a visit," Mama explained, "you'll ride the Red Ball bus from Russellville and get off here. My Uncle George Sutton will be driving. You know him. He won't let you miss your stop. Just be sure and write us ahead of time so your Daddy can be here to meet you."

Mama got Daddy — who seldom got in a hurry about anything — going again. Ten miles down Hwy 7, he stopped at Andy Anderson's General Store. "Gotta check with ole Andy on some bluetick pups," he said.

Mama told me to stay in the cab with her and the girls. When Daddy didn't come out right away, she sent me in after him. He and Andy were still talking dogs. "Them pups are owned by a man down on Richland Creek," he told Daddy. "Lonzo Hawkins the moonshiner can give you directions to the feller's place."

While I stood waiting to get in a word for Mama, a pretty blonde with shoulder-length curls came tripping in from the back and introduced herself as Jeri Lynn Anderson. She didn't wait for me to give my name. "Yer James Carl, the boy wonder from Mt. Judy. Air ye on yer way to Tech?"

I nodded, a bit captivated. None of the girls at Judy had ever called me a boy wonder. "Yep," I said. "Tech's whar' we're bound."

"I'm startin' there myself," Jeri Lynn noted. "Daddy's taking me down early in the mornin'."

Mama's voice rang out. "Fred? James Carl?"

"Wal, Andy," Daddy finished, "if you see thet feller from Richland, tell 'em I might be interested in buyin' his pups."

"Fred?"

"We're comin', Hester. Let's go, son."

I waved jauntily back at Jeri Lynn. "See ya at Tech."

Russellville was 40 more miles south. I knew the road well from going on buying trips with Daddy.

The Model A carried us down the dusty highway and along the ridge of a mountain where the road descended into Bullfrog Valley. Part way down, a squirrel ran across the road in front of the truck.

Daddy jammed on the brakes, grabbed his .22 rifle from the back of the cab. I started to get out, but Mama pulled me back.

The rifle cracked twice. "Got two of 'um," Daddy yelled triumphantly. He emerged from the woods and tossed the red fox squirrels into the back of the truck.

Daddy cranked the Model A again. Down the mountain and into the valley we puttered. Crossing through Booger Holler we chugged onto the bridge that spanned Illinois Bayou. A mile down the road from where we hit the pavement, we rolled into Dover where Doc Sexton now had his office. Daddy wanted to stop and say hello to Doc. Mama said, "No, we're goin' on. We'll be after dark gettin' home."

A little farther on we passed a Baptist church named Shiloh, then a sign saying, **WELCOME TO RUSSELLVILLE, Population 8,166**. We crossed a narrow bridge over a little creek. "We're comin' in to Tech!" I squealed as the Model A clattered down El Paso Avenue through the middle of the grassy campus.

A loud roar filled our ears. My heart skipped a beat. "What in the world?" declared Mama in alarm.

Daddy pointed to two planes taking off, one a few hundred feet beyond the other. "Military planes," Daddy shouted. "They're trainin' pilots over thar."

He pulled the Model A to the curb so we could watch. Not until the planes flew into a fluffy white cloud did Daddy ease the truck back into the street.

I'd seen in the Tech catalog a campus map with pictures of the buildings. "That's the basketball gym on the left," I announced to Mama. "And Bailey Hall, the science building, is jist across the street. Look,

Mama, there's Wilson Dorm where the boys live. It's built like a U. And there's the big administration building. Look at them big white columns in front. Can we stop and look around?" My heart was pounding.

"You'll have plenty of time tomorrow," Mama assured. "Right now we're taking you to my cousin Jane's house on L Street."

A strong female voice rang out. "Forward, march. To the right, march. Companeeeee, halt!" Daddy jerked the truck to a surprised stop. We looked to our left and saw a column of women soldiers standing at attention. Mama's eyes got big. "They're training girls to go off to war," she said. "It just don't seem right."

"Forward, march!" The column of WACs headed toward the airport. Daddy started the truck up once again. Turning left at the athletic field, he putted over to Arkansas Avenue and made a right, then another left and we were on L Street. A half mile further on, he pulled up to a neat, white bungalow. "This is where my cousin Jane and her man, George, live," Mama announced. "This is where you'll be boardin'."

We were barely out of the truck when a buxom, white-haired lady came trotting out of the house. She hugged Mama, kissed little Jimmie and Freddie, shook hands with Daddy, then patted me on my black head. "You must be my little boarder." I pulled myself up to my full five feet four inches, hoping for a little more respect.

"George won't be home from work for over an hour. Hope you all can stay for supper."

"We'd love to," Mama said, "but I told Gussie

we'd be back before sundown. She's taking care of the twins."

"Well, then," Aunt Jane said. "I still need to fix you all a little somethin' to eat, so you won't get hungry on the road."

Aunt Jane served us sandwiches. Mama then pulled me aside and presented directions for the next day. "Just stay on L street 'til you get to Arkansas, turn right and you'll see the big administration building across from the football field. They should have gotten your application and high school report card by now."

Mama reached into her pocketbook and handed me a check already made out to Tech for $45. "That oughta be enough for your tuition and dinners in the dining hall. If it's more than that, tell them to mail us a statement."

She passed me a $10 bill. "That should cover your books, with a little extra left over for treats. I put two notebooks and six pencils in with your clothes. You've got a fountain pen in your shirt pocket. If you need money for anything else, ask Jane. I'll pay her back."

Daddy walked over to the truck bed and pulled out the dead squirrels. "Kilt 'em on the way down," he told Jane proudly. "You kin cook 'em fer supper. James Carl likes the brains."

Daddy eyed his pocket watch. "We'd best be gettin' on the road."

Mama quickly gave instructions to Aunt Jane. "Make him mind just like he was your own boy. Don't let him listen to the radio or go out and play until he does his lessons."

She turned back to me. "And James Carl, remember Russellville isn't Judy. Watch out for cars when you're ridin' your bicycle. Study your lessons and get to bed before nine o'clock at night."

Mama's eyes were reddening. "Oh, Lord," she bawled, "it's so hard to leave you, James Carl."

She pulled me close. "You're so little and so young, comin' to the city. I don't know if I can stand havin' you so far away."

"Aw, I'll be okay, Mama. Aunt Jane will take good care of me." I steeled myself to keep from crying, too.

"I know she will, son, but it's still awful, awful hard for me." Mama wiped her face with the tail of the old sweater she was wearing.

Daddy's eyes were watering, but he didn't break up. He just took my hand and said, "You be a good boy, Son. Come home any weekend you want to. Just write us and let us know when to meet the Red Ball at Lurton. We'll go fishin', then take the dogs out and catch a coon."

Mama looked at me, then Jane. "See that he combs his hair and washes his face before goin' to class."

Daddy pulled at Mama's sweater. "Aw, he knows that, Hester. He ain't a baby no more." Daddy helped Jimmie and Freddie back into the truck and motioned to Mama. "Let's go, Hester. It's gettin' late. Mah dawgs'll be starvin'."

Mama grabbed me for a final goodbye kiss. "I'm real proud of you, Son," she managed in a quivering voice. Finally, she got in the truck where Jimmie and Freddie were wiggling beside Daddy.

Jimmie began wailing. "Ain't James Carl comin' home with us?"

"He'll be up fer a visit soon," Daddy assured.

Daddy pulled out into the dirt street. Mama, her eyes still running over, looked back and waved at me and "Aunt" Jane. Except to stay overnight with kinfolks in Big Creek Valley, I'd never spent a night away from home. Forty years later Mama would recall that leaving me that day was the hardest thing she ever did.

I stood watching until the Model A disappeared in a cloud of dust down L Street. "Come on and I'll show you your room," Aunt Jane urged. Opening my suitcase, she hung my Sears & Roebuck suit and matching brown necktie in a closet. "You can put your other things in the dresser," she said.

I had two pairs of overalls (including the ones I had on), two pairs of khaki pants, three denim shirts, one dress shirt, two pairs of thick socks, and one change of winter long-handles.

"Don't you have any summer underwear?" Aunt Jane asked.

My face reddened. "I, uh, don't need any."

"You just sleep in your shirt tail?"

"Yes'um."

"I'll buy you two pairs when I go to the store Saturday," she said. "Your mama will pay me back."

"Yes'um."

"Uh, will you wear your long-handles tomorrow?"

"I'll go in my shirt tail. Won't nobody know." My face was still red. I felt uncomfortable talking with this lady about underwear, even if she was Mama's cousin.

"You can wear a pair of George's shorts," Aunt Jane said. "I'll pin them up so they won't fall down. That way you won't be embarrassed if you have to strip for a physical exam."

"Yes'um," was all I could say.

That ordeal over, we walked out onto the porch. I asked her if I could look around the neighborhood. "I'm like my daddy, Aunt Jane. I don't like to be cooped up long in one place."

"Well, don't go far," she ordered. "George will be home in a little while and we'll have supper."

My feet felt cramped. When Aunt Jane went in the house I slipped off my shoes and hid them under the porch. Strolling east along the dirt street I came to a little creek. I slipped down the bank to the upper end of a shallow pool and turned over a rock. Two big red-backed crawdads backed out. I picked them up and shoved them into my right pocket. Turning over other rocks, I pocketed three more.

"Whatcha got there?" I looked up and saw a cotton-headed, freckled-faced boy, staring down from the clay bank. He looked about 11 or 12.

I held up one of the red-backed crawdads and grinned. "Caught four more this big." He slid down the bank and introduced himself as Lem Holly who lived "back down the road a ways." I gave him my name, adding, "I'm staying with Mr. and Mrs. Essex."

He puffed out his chest a bit. "I'm in the sixth grade. What 'er you in?"

"I'm enrollin' at Tech tomorrow."

He eyed me suspiciously. "You some kind of midget?"

"I'm 13. Back in Mt. Judy, they call me 'Fesser, short for professer."

He still didn't believe I was going to college. "You have to graduate from high school to go to Tech."

"I graduated last week."

Lem's eyes showed his incredulity.

I pinched off two crawdad tails and popped the raw meat in my mouth.

Lem's eyes lit up. "Wowzie! I ain't never seen nobody eat a crawdad tail before."

"You oughta try one." I pinched off another tail.

"Unhuh," Lem said. "I'd better get home. See ya."

I walked back to my boarding house. George Essex was home from work.

While Aunt Jane cooked supper, "Uncle" George and I sat in the porch swing and got acquainted. "I know all of yer mama's Sutton family," Uncle George said. "Her Grandpa Simon Solomon Sutton was the doctor on our side of Big Creek. Doc Sutton has been dead 12 or 15 years now. He and Aunt Mary Ann are buried between some cedars, right down the hill from his old place."

"I've been there," I noted. "Mama would like me to be a doctor like her grandpa."

"So you'll be taking a pre-med major?"

"Mama says I don't have to decide on that this quarter. I might end up majorin' in business."

Aunt Jane's voice rang out, "Supper time!"

Aunt Jane had fried the squirrels and saved me the skulls. I had just cracked one open when we heard a knock. "Open the door and walk in," Uncle George instructed.

Lem, the boy I'd met at the little creek, edged into the kitchen. As I introduced him to Aunt Jane and Uncle George, his eyes widened. "Golly! You eat squirrel brains, too?"

"Have some supper with us, Lem." Aunt Jane invited. "We've got apple pie for desert."

Lem stayed for the pie. He thanked Aunt Jane, then glanced over at me. "Wanna come over and shoot some marbles at my house?"

Aunt Jane nodded. "Go on with Lem, James Carl, but be home by eight o'clock. You've got a big day comin' up tomorrow."

I grinned back at Aunt Jane. "Yes'um, I reckon I have."

When I got "home" from shooting marbles with Lem, Aunt Jane took one sniff and directed me to the bathroom. "But — but," I sputtered, "Mama doesn't make me wash off at home. I wash in the creek when the water's warm."

"Where do you wash in cold weather?" she asked.

"I wash my face and feet in a pan."

"And the rest of you?"

"I wait 'til the creek gets warm."

Aunt Jane passed me one of Uncle George's old shirts for a bathrobe. "We've got warm water in this house. You'll shower before you go to bed. Let's go into the bathroom. I'll show you how to turn the water on."

The first indoor shower of my life felt good all over. Aunt Jane hadn't mentioned soap, so I didn't use any, but I liked getting wet. That night I slept like a flint rock in a sandbar.

Chapter 4

"Registration"

I had just hooked a lunker bass in the Rock Hole, when the little alarm clock on the table beside my bed jangled me out of dreamland. I was in Russellville. Today I would sign up for classes at Tech. I felt goose bumps all over.

A soft knock came on the door. "James Carl? Can I come in?"

"Yes 'um." I pulled the covers up to my chin.

"George has already left for work. I let you sleep as long as I could." She pulled my $8.98 tweed from the closet. "You need to look good on your first day. Put this on with your dress shirt while I get your breakfast on the table."

The smell of bacon frying gave me added incentive. Dutifully clothed, I trotted into the kitchen where she motioned me to a chair. "Just help yourself," she instructed. I did. She passed me the funnies from the *Arkansas Gazette*. My kind of college mama.

Ring, ring. "Excuse me, James Carl." Aunt Jane trotted into the living room and began talking as if someone were there. Then it dawned on me that she must be talking on a telephone. I had never used one, although I had heard a phone ring on radio dramas.

"That was George," she reported, "callin' to say he has to work late tonight. I'm glad you'll be here to keep me company."

When I finished breakfast, Aunt Jane checked me over from stem to stern. "Your suit looks fine, and I guess you can go without a necktie. But your hair is a rat's nest. Don't you ever use a comb?"

"Yes'um, but I lost it. Must have drapped out of my shirt pocket yesterday when I bent down to catch a crawdad."

She darted into her bedroom and came back. "Take this red one."

I gave my hair a few rakes and slipped the comb in my pocket. Aunt Jane continued to eye my hair with displeasure. "One side's cut higher than the other," she observed. "You look like a Mohawk Indian. James Carl, who cuts your hair?"

"Daddy. He's the barber in Judy. He ain't never had no trainin', I reckon."

"Well, you're going to a professional barber when your hair grows out. Even if I have to pay for it myself. Now get along to Tech and get your class schedule lined out. Tomorrow, you'll start classes."

With Mama's check stuffed in my billfold, I jumped on my bike and began pedalling down L street toward Arkansas Avenue. Lem was coming out of his house with a book bag. "Meet you at the creek after school," he hollered. All too soon I was wheeling into the parking area in front of the enormous, white-columned, Ole Main.

Two young men stood on the steps eying me skeptically. The tall redhead held a sign reading, **AGRI**. The short, stocky one hoisted a placard labeled, **ENGINEER**. From reading the catalog I knew that these were the two biggest clubs on campus.

"Which professor's kid are you?" the redhead asked with a condescending smirk.

"No one's," I said, grinning up at them.

"This is the college, not the high school.," the engineer responded.

"I know. I've done graduated from high school," I said, proudly puffing out my scrawny chest. "Where do I go first?"

"Go through that door," the Agri boy snickered, "and get in the first line you see. That'll take you to Mr. Turpentine's desk. You start with him."

I trotted into the imposing building and found a long line of students, mostly girls. They kept staring at me and whispering to each other. Two long hours later I was standing before a sleepy-eyed man, perched behind a ponderous, wooden desk. The name plate read: "G.R. Turrentine. Registrar."

He extended his hand. "You must be the 13-year-old from Mt. Judy."

He knew how to pronounce the name of my home town. "Pleased to meetcha Mr. Turrentine."

His assistant, a trim, blonde woman seated before a typewriter at a side desk, tossed me a smile. "We've been eagerly anticipating your arrival." My thin chest swelled. She held up the application and the grade certification I had mailed.

Mr. Turrentine motioned for me to take a chair. "Will you be staying in Wilson Hall? That's the men's dorm."

"I'm, uh livin' with relatives."

"Good, good. You're a little young to be in with our men."

"Uh, how do I sign up for classes?" I asked.

"You didn't receive instructions in the mail?"

"No, sir. The mail don't get through to Judy when the creeks air up."

Mr. Turrentine grimaced. "Doesn't instead of don't. Are, not air," the blonde lady corrected.

"Did your parents give you a check?" Mr. Turrentine wondered.

"Mama did. She got the figures from the Tech catalog."

The blonde lady handed me a form. "Fill this out and take it to the business office over there. They'll take your mama's check, too."

I wrote down James Carl Hefley, Mt. Judea, Arkansas and puzzled over what to put down as my major. I didn't want agriculture. Engineering sounded scary. I wasn't sure I could make it in science. I didn't see pre-med. Finally I wrote "business," thinking I could change to the doctoring track later.

I puzzled over "church preference."

"Having trouble?" the blonde asked. Mr. Turrentine was busy with a girl who had come up behind me.

I pointed to the church question. "Mama and

Daddy don't go to any church regular. Uncle Bill Hefley is big in the Church of Christ. Uncle Dan Hefley's a Holiness preacher. Aunt Lucy's a Jehovah's Witness. Uncle — "

"Well, what are you?" she grinned.

"Nothin', I guess."

"Then just put down 'none' and go see Mr. Young. Oh, by the way, if you decide to move to the dorm, you'll be required to attend church on Sunday morning. The Baptist, Methodist, and Christian churches all run buses."

"Yes'um. I'll go see Mr. Young now."

I sweated out the line leading through the door of the business office. The nameplate on the counter inside announced: ROBERT A. YOUNG, BUSINESS MANAGER. Rows and rows of dorm keys hung on a side wall.

The tall, skinny, blond boy in front of me looked worried when he came to pay. "Mah name is Joshua John Brown," he reported. "I'm from up north of Dover, 'bout three miles out from Hector. Them that know me call me Josh. Uh, I've only got $12," he told Mr. Young, a smiling man with a rim of whitening hair. "But I'm willing to work."

Mr. Young asked the obvious: "You a farm boy, son?"

"Yessir, but air corn didn't git enough rain last year. Mama and Papa didn't have the money to send me to college. I told them I was goin' anyway."

Mr. Young smiled reassuringly. "Give me the $12 and go see Mr. Tomlinson. He'll give you some cows to milk or some other job at the Red Barn.

Down that hall and first door to the right. Wait, there he is, just passing my door." The business manager pointed to a skinny little man in a blue serge suit, holding a lighted cigarette between his fingers. "Go see him and get a work assignment. Bring that back to me and I'll approve your account. Then you can get on with your class selections."

Josh disappeared down the hall. Mr. Young looked at me in seeming recognition. "You must be the little kid from Mt. Judy."

"Yessir, I'm James Carl Hefley." I handed him the form given me by Mr. Turrentine's helper and Mama's $45 check. "I'm livin' in Russellville with Mama's cousin," I told him. "But I'll be eatin' dinner here."

He tallied up my fees, including a noon meal ticket and excluding a dorm room. "Comes to $45 for the term. Let's see. Your mother wrote the check for that exact amount. She must be good at accounts."

"Yessir. She keeps our store. Daddy deals in coon dogs."

Mr. Young chuckled over that. "So you're a coon hunter's boy."

"Yessir. But fishin's mah favorite sport."

The students behind me were shuffling their feet in impatience. "The next person to see is your faculty adviser," the finance man said. "That's Mr. DuLaney, the history professor. He's in Room 201." Mr. Young gave me directions, adding, "Mr. DuLaney's just a little taller than you, with gray hair that makes him look older than he actually is."

I went to the staircase and paused. *This shore*

ain't like Juday school, I thought. *I ain't never been in a school with more than one story.*

Arriving in Room 201, I got behind two girls who were griping about the imbalance between the sexes at Tech. We started talking and exchanged names. Emma was the red-head, Marie a gum-smacking dishwater blonde. "Ah didn't know I'd be goin' to a girls' school," moaned Emma. "There must be six females to evuh male that's registerin' today. And now it looks like we'll be takin' classes with little boys as well."

"Yeah," moaned Marie. "Ain't it pitiful. Maybe we can date the Navy cadets."

"Ah've already checked on them. They're kept pretty busy with flight trainin'."

I stood twisting and fidgeting while the diminutive, prematurely gray-haired man seated behind the desk jotted down, first Emma, then Marie's courses. "Arkansas History is-is required," he told them with a slight stutter. "I-I've still got three places open. Meets every day at two o'clock, Monday through Friday. You must have it to graduate."

"Might as well git Arkansas over with," Emma sighed. "Marie and me will take two of the places left in your two o'clock class." She covered her lips and giggled. "That was jist a joke, Mr. DuLaney. I'm sure we'll love your class."

My turn came. Mr. DuLaney's eyes swept me up and down, lingering on my uneven haircut. "You're the lit-little Mt. Judy boy. All the faculty's been talking about you. Do-do you think you can cut the mustard?"

"I don't like mustard, but I can cut it if I have to."

Mr. DuLaney gave me an encouraging smile. "Mt. Judy is-is in Newton County. That's the only Republican county in the state. I guess you knew that."

"Yessir, I was told that in school. But the folks around Judy don't care much about political parties. It's who's runnin' fer sheriff and the school board. Whoever's got the most money to dish out to the voters generally gits elected."

"Buyin' votes is very sad," Mr. DuLaney lamented. "Especially when you think of so-so many young people out on the battlefields, fighting to preserve our democracy."

Buying votes was the custom back in the hills, and I had never really thought about it not being right.

He looked down at my schedule sheet. "You want the last seat in my two o'clock class? You'll be in there with the two girls who just left."

"Yessir."

I liked this little man with the slight stutter. "What else do you teach, Mr. DuLaney?"

"European History is one of my courses. Would you like to take it? It-it isn't required for a business major, but you'll get a better understanding of how this terrible war got started."

"You can sign me up."

"Very good. Now let's work out the rest of-of your schedule. Friday afternoon Phys. Ed., under Mr. Paul Fiser, is mandatory for all freshman boys. Mr. Fiser is also in charge of our food service. Now another required course is Composition and

Rhetoric, taught by Miss Lillian Massie. She-she's the English authority around here. Keeps us all on our t-t-toes. Her class meets upstairs in Room 302, but she's meeting students over to my right."

He pointed across the room at a stern-looking, straight-backed lady whose brown hair was braided and wrapped around her head. I felt a dark sense of foreboding.

"Now you'll need at least one class in your major field. You can take other courses in business later. That is your chosen field, isn't it?"

"Yeah, I guess so. Mama, I think, would rather I study to be a doctor. Her grandpa on her mama's side was Doctor Simon Solomon Sutton. He died the year after I was born."

"Well, you can always switch to science. That's pre-med."

I fingered a listing in the college catalog open before us. "Typewriting. I'd like to learn how to type."

Mr. DuLaney dutifully put down Elementary Typewriting. "Miss Dorothy Clark will be your teacher. She's an experienced secretary." He pursed his lips. "Not many boys take typing. You'll be-be in there with a room full of girls."

The little professor ran his eye down my card. "You've got four classes Monday-Wednesday-Friday, and Arkansas History Monday through Friday. Then Phys. Ed. with Mr. Fiser on Friday at four o'clock." He eyed me with some concern. "Think you can keep awake on your heavy days? Think you can discipline yourself to spend time in the library on your low class days?"

I nodded confidently. "Sure."

I pulled out my dollar pocket watch saved from my sales project in the store. Mr. DuLaney eyed the time piece in my hand. "It-it's getting close to lunch time. The dining hall is right behind this building and across the lawn. You'll see the students going in. But first you need to go in Mr. Crabaugh's office and have him give a final okay to your class schedule. Mr. Crabaugh is our academic dean."

"What's lunch?" I asked, puzzled.

"That's the noon meal," Mr. DuLaney responded with a kind smile.

"Oh, ya means dinner. Thanks, uh, I hope that won't take long. I'm as hongry as a starved possum."

An audible gasp issued from across the room. Miss Massie, the English teacher, was shaking her head grimly. Had she heard me?

I didn't go by her desk to ask.

The trip to Dean Crabaugh's office took less than five minutes. His secretary stamped my class schedule. Mr. Crabaugh, a keen-eyed man with curly brown hair, pumped my right hand vigorously. Somehow he knew my name without looking at the paper. "We're all pleased that you chose Tech, James. Our doors are open to you. We'll do our best to give you a real learning experience."

Stomach growling, I had just stepped into the hall when I felt a tap on my skinny shoulder. "Mr. James Carl Hefley?"

I turned to see a skinny brunette with pen and notebook. "You're quite a celebrity on campus," she said. "I'm a reporter for the *Arka-Tech* student paper. May I interview you for a story?"

Boy, howdy. I'd never felt so important in all my life. I suddenly forgot my hunger pangs. "Why, shore."

I followed the reporter into a vacant classroom.

"Are you really just 13 years old?" she asked.

I nodded, adding, "But I'll be 14 come June second."

"When did you graduate from high school?"

I counted back. "Nine days ago. Mama set me on two pillows so's ever'body could see me." I asked a question: "Am I really the youngest student ever to enter college here?"

"Mr. Turrentine isn't sure. He says you're probably one of the youngest."

That took a little air out of my tires.

"Mr. Turrentine heard of one boy who was so short that only a part of his head could be seen over the counter at the Business Office."

"I could see Mr. Young pretty well. Mama measured me before I left home and she says I'm five feet four inches tall. The scales in the feed room of our store weighed me out at 110 pounds."

She kept asking questions and making notes. She wrote in her story that I began my "formal education" in the eighth grade at Mt. Judea, "in a rural section of Newton County where schools were as few as Democrats." She didn't ask if I'd attended any one-room schools.

When she finished, I could tell that she was impressed. "Well, thank you very much, Mr. James

Carl Hefley. I'm sure you'll go a long way in life."

After the interview, she walked with me over to the noisy dining hall, then excused herself to talk to a boy at a nearby table.

Josh Brown, the boy in front of me at the business office, was just ahead of me in line again. "I've never et in a place with this many people," he remarked.

"Yeah, an' all of 'em jabberin' at onct."

We saw the others grabbing trays and silverware, so we followed suit. "Gimme a big bunch of taters," I told the first girl behind the counter. "I'm starvin'."

Josh asked for big helpings, too. We laughed and made jokes with the girl servers as we moved forward. Coming off the end of the chow line, I heard a deep voice that sounded like Andy from the radio show, "Amos and Andy." I looked over and saw a beefy black man under a tall, puffy, white hat, giving orders to the kitchen crew. "Hurry up with dem taters. Git some mo cherry pie out heah. These people are starvin'."

I stopped and stared. And stared. On grocery buying trips to Russellville, I'd seen a few blacks at a distance, but I'd never seen one up close. Not in Big Creek Valley or in all of Newton County. Not in Harrison, either.

The students behind could see that I had stopped and had fixed my eyes on the stout black man who wore a little tag identifying himself as Joe Sidney. "Whut's the holdup?" a boy yelled. "Ain't yuh nevah seen a nigguh before?"

Josh gave me a little shove, breaking my concentration. Still curious, I decided I'd come back later to get a longer look at Joe Sidney. We were just picking up our trays when I heard a familiar voice. "Hey, 'Fesser, over here."

I looked over to see C.B. Hudson and Junior Johnson, my classmates from Judy.

Josh followed me over to their table. C.B. said he and Junior had already moved into Wilson Hall. "Most of the boys living there are cadets," he said.

We went through the routine of asking, "What are you takin'?" The four of us would be together for Phys. Ed., Composition and Rhetoric and Arkansas History.

"An' I got interviewed by a reporter from the *Arka-Tech*." I blurted. "She asked me my literary favorites."

Junior almost choked. "I didn't know you had any. What'd ya tell her?"

"I said I liked 'Jitters.' "

"What's 'Jitters?' " Josh asked with a perfectly straight face.

I decided to show off my learning. "A comic strip. I read it this morning in the *Arkansas Gazette* for the first time."

"Oh," was all Joshua said. I later learned he had never read the state's leading newspaper.

A familiar voice pealed out from the table in back of us. I turned to see Jeri Lynn, taking a seat beside a broad-shouldered, golden-haired boy.

She smiled back. "Well, hi there James Carl and C.B. and Junior. Who's that fella with you?"

Josh blushed red when I introduced him. He couldn't think of a word to say.

"Jeri Lynn won't bite you," I assured him. "She's a real country girl."

"And good lookin' too," Josh mumbled under his breath. He was smitten.

C.B. and Junior finished eating first. "We're goin' over to the gym and shoot a few goals," C.B. said. "Gotta stay in shape if we're gonna make the basketball team this fall."

"Maybe I'll come by and shoot a few with you," I ventured.

"Yeah," Junior said. "See you there."

Josh picked up his tray. "I've gotta be out at the Red Barn by 1:30. Mr. Tomlinson's got a job fer me." He cast a shy glance at Jeri Lynn. She caught it and grinned back. Josh blushed fiercely again. Unable to speak, he got in line to dump his dirty dishes.

I moseyed over to Jeri Lynn's table. She introduced me to Howie Parish. "Howie's a super basketball player," she said. "You'll be hearin' about him when the season opens."

I saw the black cook heading toward a side door. "Nice to see you again, Jeri Lynn an' ta meetcha, Howie," I said. "I'm gonna hoof around the campus."

Stricken with curiosity, I followed the black man, Joe Sidney out the door, keeping about ten paces behind. He never looked back.

He turned right at the gymnasium; so did I. When he slipped into the little cafe in front of the gym, called the Techionery, I was right behind him. I had read about the Techionery in the college catalog, but this was my first time to see the student hangout.

"Gonna take a sentimental journey...." Two

couples were shuffling cheek to cheek around the kitchen-sized floor space between the booths and the counter.

The black cook was parked in a booth with three white boys, all jabbering like old buddies. I plopped down on a stool and just sat there, staring at him.

"Yuh want somethin' to eat?" the giggly girl behind the counter asked me.

"No thanks. I'm jist lookin' around."

Doris Day finished her "Sentimental Journey." A boy pushed in another nickel.

"...He's the Boogie-Woogie Bugle Boy of Company B!" the Andrew Sisters announced.

The place came alive with dancers, swinging and swaying and singing the tune. A tall gal pulled me up and swung me around. I ducked under her arm and skittered out the side door that led into the gym.

C.B. and Junior were shooting baskets with Jeri Lynn's big-muscled friend.

C.B. hollered at me. "C'mon, 'Fesser. Two on two, let's have a 20-point game. You can be Howie's partner."

I'd seen C.B. and Junior play on the dirt court in front of Judy School. They weren't real tall, but they made up for height with accuracy in shooting.

I jerked off my suit coat. What fun. In a 20-point game, C.B. and Junior beat us only by four. I even made one goal with a wild shot that C.B. failed to bat away.

Howie Parish swatted me on the back and suggested, "Hefley, for a little kid you're not half bad. You oughta try out for basketball this fall. With

63

so many boys in the service, Coach Tucker will have slim pickin's."

I glanced at C.B. and Junior for encouragement. Both nodded, which I took for a recommendation.

"Hey, yeah, maybe I will." After the interview for the *Arka-Tech* I was willing to try anything.

C.B., Junior and Howie went back to their dorm rooms. I dribbled around for a few minutes, then walked over to the dorm myself. Mama didn't know it yet, but I was planning on moving there when the fall term started.

Wilson Hall, I'd read in the catalog, had been formed by connecting two older dorms to make a U. A flag waved from a tall metal pole between the two wings. Dorm parents — faculty couples — had apartments at both ends of the U.

I discovered the dorm lounge. It was full and running over with blue-uniformed Navy cadets, playing cards, shooting dice and batting pingpong balls about.

A tall hawk-nosed cadet looked at me sourly as I entered. "Youse a faculty kid?" He sounded like a young Jimmy Durante.

"I'm a Tech student."

"Ya don't look like one. If ya are, ya'll still have to leave. This lounge is off limits to civilians."

"Even college boys who live in the dorm?"

"Yeah, especially guys in the dorm."

"That ain't fair."

"Durante" and about five others began advancing toward me. I turned tail and ran.

It was time to go home anyway. I jumped on my

bike, left parked in front of Ole Main, zipped back to Aunt Jane's house, stripped off my scratchy tweed suit, stepped into a comfortable pair of overalls and headed for the creek. I hadn't been there ten minutes when Lem and another 12-year-old named Rudy got there. Lem told Rudy I was a student at Tech. "But he don't act like the college guys," Lem added. "He catches crawdads and eats their tails. An' he eats squirrel brains, too."

Rudy had to see me eat crawdad tails.

We waded down to the place where I'd caught crawdads the afternoon before. I picked up a big one, ripped off its tail, and shoved the white meat in my mouth. Rudy was properly impressed.

Moving from one hole to another and turning over rocks, I soon filled my pockets. Lem and Rudy even demonstrated their bravery by catching a few to take home and show their parents.

I carried two pocketsful back to Aunt Jane's house. She took one look and laid down the law. "Out! Take those creatures back to the creek!"

I quickly backed out of the house and found an old coffee can in the yard. I filled it with a water hose and dropped in the crawdads.

"James Carl!" I whirled around to see a grim-faced Aunt Jane standing on the porch. "Didn't I tell you to take those creatures back to the creek."

"Yes'um, but can't I keep 'em under the porch tonight?"

"Then what?" she demanded.

"I'll take 'em with me to Tech. I'll have fun scarin' girls."

She shouted at me. "JAMES CARL! You are in college now. Go pitch those ugly creatures back in the creek, or I'll — I'll write your mother to come and get you."

I did what she asked. Then I sat down and wrote a letter myself:

> Dear Mama and Daddy:
> I miss you. There ain't nothing for me to do in Russellville this weekend, except go to a fancy church. I'd rather come home and see you.
> I'll ride the Red Ball to Lurton Saturday and you can meet me there. I'll come back to Tech on the Red Ball Sunday evening."
> Your college boy,
> James Carl
> P.S. Aunt Jane and Uncle George are treating me real good. I'm signed up for five classes at Tech.

Chapter 5

"First Daze"

I rolled out of bed Wednesday morning, pulled on a pair of overalls and bounced into the kitchen where Aunt Jane had breakfast waiting.

She frowned at my garb. "You look like a hick in those overalls. After breakfast, go put on some pants for your first day of classes."

Before I could say, "Yes'um," the phone rang.

"Go ahead and eat," she instructed. "Don't wait on me." She hurried into the living room to catch the phone. She was still yakking when I put down the funnies and slipped out the door. My mind was on "Li'l Abner" and I forgot to change to pants.

I pulled up to Ole Main, parked my bike, and ran into the building and up the stairs to Room 302. Four other early birds, all girls, were chattering in Miss Massie's classroom when I plunked my little behind into a back row seat. The room was fast filling up when Jeri Lynn Anderson, looking like Miss Country Innocence, made her grand entry. She plopped down beside me and breathed into my ear. "A girl who had Miss Massie last year told me she's awful. I sure wish her class wasn't required."

Josh framed the door. I waved him over. Jeri Lynn smiled at him and he blushed. "Had to milk 12 cows this mornin'," he explained as he took a place on the other side of me.

Howie Parish parked himself directly in front of us. He turned around to say hi to Jeri Lynn, then winked at me. "Hey, Hefley, ya goin' to the freshman dance tonight? There'll be a lot of purty girls there."

"Nah, I ain't goin' to no dance tonight. And — "

All eyes turned to the classroom door. There she was, the feared Professor Lillian Massie, groomed like a society lady. Without a word or a trace of a smile, she eased her slim frame into the teacher's chair, pulled a long, black cigarette holder from her purse, tapped in a Lucky Strike and announced ceremoniously, "Good morning, young men and women."

She flipped a flame from a silver lighter, lit the Lucky, and raised her right hand in the air — "like the Statue of Liberty," Howie Parish said later, "holdin' up her torch to show her freedom." As the smoke trailed across the musty room, the girl next to Howie coughed nervously. Nobody laughed.

Miss Massie's eyes coolly surveyed the room, then spoke with the soft huskiness of Lauren Bacall in the movie, "To Have and To Have Not." "Let us first take care of some preliminaries. I am Lillian Massie," she announced, as if we didn't already know. "I am a woman, as must be evident to you by now. You may address me as 'Miss' or 'Professor Massie.'

"I will give you a little biographical information on myself so you may be better informed.

"I am the only child of devoted parents who live in Fayetteville where my father is a professor of mathematics at the University." Miss Massie's eyes swept the room to see if we were all listening.

"In the summer of 1932, President Hull and Mr. Crabaugh motored up to Fayetteville and interviewed me for a vacancy in the English department here. I had previously taught in such illustrious places as Ardmore, Oklahoma; Farmington, Arkansas; and Klein, Montana. I had also worked as a purchasing agent, an abstracter, and in an electrical testing laboratory. The latter may be the reason some consider me a shocking person."

A yawn erupted from beside me. "Am I boring you, Mr. Joshua Brown?" she asked laconically.

Josh came fully awake, surprised that she knew his name. "Oh, yes, I mean, no ma'am."

"Then permit me to continue. President Hull and Mr. Crabaugh must have been short on prospects, for they invited me to join them at this institution. I have now been on the faculty at dear old Arkansas Polytechnic College for twelve years, and, I hope, have gained a reputation for fairness." She paused to take a drag on her Lucky. "No matter what you may have heard, I have given an occasional 'A' grade. I've also awarded a few 'Fs' to worthy recipients."

She took another long drag on her Lucky, casting her gaze around the smoky room before resuming. "I've also invited an occasional student to drop out of my class before he or she receives a failing grade.

If one of you should prove yourself worthy of an F, I will empathize with you, but I'll still give it to you.

"Miss Jones of the psychology department and I volunteered for the Women's Army Corps to help the war effort. We endured the rigors and indignities of physical examinations and were duly pronounced '4-F' — unfit for service.

"Now that I've told you my life story, please let me assure you that you will have equal time, as opportunities arise for sharing your life experiences. I will now proceed to call the roll. Please answer 'here' if you are present and correct me if I mispronounce your name."

"Adams, Mr. Harry Adams."

"Present, Miss Massie."

"You need not announce my name each time. 'Present' will suffice."

Fixing her gaze, she nodded gravely as each student answered, Upon calling my name, she added an unsettling comment. "Mr. James Carl Hefley, as I was coming into this class, I heard you say, 'I'm not goin' to no dance tonight.' That, Mr. Hefley, is a double negative and will not be tolerated. Not even from a young man who dresses like a clod. Is that understood?"

Keenly aware of my blue denim overalls, I dropped my head, not daring to look her in the eye, and mumbled, "Yes'um." I didn't have the grit to ask her what a double negative was.

She held her stare. "You're in college now. You shall learn to speak and write proper English. Or you will receive a failing grade in this course."

Her eyes again swept the room. "That applies to every member of this class."

She pulled a book from her case. "This text is available in the Techionery for one dollar and ninety-five cents. When we meet next on Friday morning, each of you will have a copy.

"You may have heard that I am a difficult teacher," she continued. "Not really. Not for those who wish to become cultured ladies and gentlemen. You may have received the impression that I was picking on Mr. Hefley, the young man in overalls. I assure you that I had only his best interests at heart."

She managed a faint smile. "Like everyone else, I have my personal likes and dislikes. It has been said that I prefer young men to young women. That is true. I assure you, however, that I will not let my personal preferences prevent fairness in grading.

"The name of this class, as listed in the college catalog, is Composition and Rhetoric." She cast her eyes around the classroom. I shrank down in my seat. "Miss Marshall, please favor us with a definition of composition."

"C-c-composition," the girl stuttered, "is the way you put things together."

Miss Massie smiled faintly. "That's a start, Miss Marshall."

Miss Massie glanced down at her roll book. "Mr. Howard Parish, this is your chance to shine."

"Composition is the act of combining parts to form a whole."

"Excellent, Mr. Parish. Where did you find that?"

"In my dictionary this morning. I thought you

might ask. Well, uh, to be truthful, a student who was here last year told me you'd start with definitions. So I did some memorizing."

Miss Massie extended her smile. "I perceive that you will be one of my better students."

A rough whisper from Josh scratched my ear. "Teacher's pet."

Miss Massie must have seen Josh's lips moving. "Mr. Brown, you will refrain from talking to a fellow student, except when such communication is deemed appropriate by me."

She cued in on Marie, one of the girls I had met at registration. "Miss Madison, please pronounce rhetoric for us."

"Reh-toric."

"Ret'er ik," Miss Massie corrected. "Spelled r-h-e-t-o-r-i-c as it appears on the cover of your textbook."

Miss Massie focused next on Emma Harper, lounging next to Marie. "Miss Harper, square your shoulders and sit up straight as a young college woman should."

Shoulders rose all around the room.

"Now that you have corrected your posture, please define rhetoric, Miss Harper."

"Rhetoric, I think, has to do with the way you speak."

Miss Massie licked her red lips. "Is there someone here who can define rhetoric more precisely?"

Howie Parish smugly spoke again. "Rhetoric is the study of the effective use of language."

"Excellent, excellent! Mr. Parish, you're even smarter than you look. Now put composition and rhetoric together and tell your fellow class members what this course is all about."

Howie spoke slowly and deliberately. "In this class we will learn to combine the parts of speech in ways that will help us write and speak correctly."

Miss Massie looked as if she could have kissed Howie right there in class. Josh covered his face with his hands to prevent her from seeing his scowl.

"Very good," Miss Massie purred. "You can expect to see that question on your first test."

She opened her text. "Those of you who already have your books, please turn to page six. Others may look on as we review the eight parts of speech."

She singled out a gum-chewing blonde near the door. "Miss Singleton, we're all aware that you can imitate a cow. Will you please put your cud away and direct your attention to the subject at hand."

The blonde's face flashed crimson.

"I see you already have a book, Miss Singleton. Turn to page six and find the definition of a noun."

The girl quickly found the page and read, "A noun is a word used to name a person, place, or thing."

Miss Massie spoke with biting sarcasm. "Miss Singleton, you didn't follow my instructions. I said, 'find the definition.' I didn't say, 'read to us the definition.' Are you in need of a hearing aid?"

The blonde blushed again. "No, Miss Massie."

"Well, next time, give your attention to what I actually said, not what you think I said."

So my first class went for the rest of the hour.

Howie and three or four others were smiling when the bell rang. Some of us looked pale, especially when she assigned nouns, pronouns and adjectives for Friday. "If you haven't purchased your text, see that you do before the sun sets," she ordered.

Josh jumped up, mumbling, "I've gotta git out and git some air."

Miss Massie must have heard him. "Sit down, Mr. Brown. I will tell you when you can go." She tapped the ashes of her cigarette into an ashtray, then tossed in the butt. She dropped the cigarette holder back in her purse. She closed her book. She stood up, her eyes again curtaining the room.

"Class dismissed."

I bolted for the door and ran down the hall to be on time for typewriting class. I had never used a typewriter before and I couldn't wait to try one out.

The room filled rapidly. I looked around and counted. Sixteen girls, me and one other boy. Each parked in front of a black Underwood office typewriter. After calling the roll and announcing the name of the textbook, Dorothy Clark, our attractive, auburn-haired instructor got down to business.

"You are here to learn how to type rapidly and correctly. The buttons in front of you are called keys. Each key carries two characters, small and capital letters, numbers, punctuation marks and other symbols.

"Now there are two ways to type. The slow way is to hunt and peck."

"Like a chicken," I chirped. "Peck, peck, peck."

Miss Clark grinned at me, lingering a bit on my

overalls. "Peck, peck, peck won't earn you many dollar bills, young man. Real bills," she said. "Not chicken bills." The class cackled. What a contrast Miss Clark was to Miss Massie.

"The second way is ten times better. You use your eight fingers and your right thumb. Come look over my shoulders as I demonstrate both methods."

We crowded around Miss Clark. Peck, peck, peck. She used only her index fingers.

She then spread both hands across the keys and typed a paragraph, her fingers flying up and down to cover the keyboard.

"Put yourself in the place of a company president. Which typist do you think he would hire for a position in his office?"

She didn't have to wait for an answer.

"Now, back to your typewriters. Roll in a sheet of paper. Place your fingers on the home keys — a-s-d-f with your left hand and j-k-l-semi-colon with your right." She pointed to a color-coded wall picture showing the correct position of each finger.

"We will start out with a series of exercises that will train your fingers to use these keys correctly. Then we will go on to the rest of the keys. Don't get impatient. We'll be typing words before you know it. Believe me, it is worth the time invested to learn to type correctly."

I dutifully began typing fjf fjf fjf fjf. Suddenly I became aware that Miss Clark was standing behind me, laughing. My fingers had slipped down and I was typing vmv vmv vmv. Miss Clark just chuckled and stepped up behind the next student.

While everybody was still smiling, she began pointing to the different parts of the typewriter. "The warning bell rings to tell you that you're at the end of the line. You have five more spaces you may use before coming to the end of the margin. Then throw the carriage back with your left hand."

I felt very awkward, but kept working to finish each line correctly. It took a while to adjust to moving the carriage back with just the right amount of force.

"Well, you've been introduced to the typewriter," she said when the bell rang. "Tomorrow we'll learn more parts of the instrument. We'll work step by step, bit by bit and when the course is over you will be accomplished typists. How you concentrate and apply yourselves will determine the grade you get in the course."

From Miss Clark's typing class, I joined the crush of students hurrying to the Little Theater on the third floor for the assembly that marked the beginning of the new school term. Once inside, I looked around for a familiar face and spotted country boy Josh Brown in a seat far back in a corner. He waved me over.

"Why are you back here all by yourself?" I asked.

" 'Cause ah'm about to fall asleep. Ah was up 'till three o'clock this mawnin' helpin' birth a calf at the Red Barn. Didn't git to bed 'til four. Wake me up when this is over."

The faculty was seated on the stage. When the bell rang, President J.W. Hull stepped sprightly to the rostrum, his balding head gleaming under an overhead spotlight.

"Good morning, ladies and gentlemen. Welcome to the 1944 spring term of Arkansas Polytechnic College. Mr. Turrentine tells me that as of ten o'clock this morning, 164 students had registered for classes. Unfortunately, for you aspiring young ladies, the great majority of these are of your fairer sex. When this terrible war is over that imbalance will be corrected when our troops come marching home."

Josh stirred. "What's he sayin'?"

"That there are more girl students than boys, 'cause so many boys are in the military."

A somber voice resounded over the speaker. I pushed Josh's head down. "The president has called on Mr. DuLaney to pray."

The little history professor rose from his seat on the stage and delivered a passionate plea for heaven-sent victory. Then Mr. Marvin Williamson, the bespectacled, dark-haired band director, asked us to stand and join him in singing Tech's alma mater.

I tugged at Josh's sleeve. "C'mon, get up and sing."

> Alma mater, alma mater
> May we lift our eyes to thee,
> May thy glory and thy honor
> Be for e'er our destiny.

I reached down and jerked Josh's hair. He came awake enough to see that everybody else was standing. He shot up.

> May thy colors green and gold
> Our loyal hearts for e'er enthrall,
> And thy mem'ry live forever
> In the hearts of us all.

We sat back down. President Hull began relating

the history of how Tech became a college.

Josh began snoring. I punched him in the ribs. He snorted. "Whut's he sayin'?"

"He's gonna give us the history of Tech. Why don't you just stay awake and listen?" I was getting a little impatient with Josh.

I tuned back to President Hull.

Josh dropped off again and stayed in dreamland until I jerked at his shirt collar. "Assembly's over. You can wake up now."

"Whut'd he say? Tell me. I don't wanna be dumb."

"And I've gotta get to European History. I don't want to start off bad with Mr. DuLaney."

"I'll walk with you. Now tell me what the president said."

With Josh towering over me, I delivered a quick digest. "Back in 1909 the state legislature divided the state into four educational districts. Russellville got the Second District school by donatin' some cash and 400 acres of land. After they started offerin' college courses, the name was changed to Arkansas Polytechnic College. From that came 'Tech'."

"Did he say anything else?"

"That we oughta appreciate the sacrifice our parents air makin' in sending us here."

"I'm working my way through," Josh mumbled.

"Yeah," I countered, "but I bet yore daddy will miss you in the field."

We were hoofing down the stairs of Ole Main when I suddenly remembered something else Josh needed to know.

"President Hull said our parents had made the college responsible for our care and education. Those who live in the dorms have to be in their rooms by a certain hour, girls by seven thirty, boys by nine o'clock, unless they're workin' at the barn. And ever'body livin' on campus is supposed to go to church on Sunday. I live out in town," I said smugly. "So I don't have to go to church unless I want to.

"Oh, one more thing. Absolutely no booze. I agree with that," I said smugly. "Jist don't make me go to some fancy church."

I stopped before Room 201 and checked my class card. "This is European History. Comin' with me? I'll keep ya awake."

"Nah," Josh said. "I didn't sign up fer this furrin' stuff. See you in Arkansas History at two." He looked up at the room number. "It meets heah, too."

European History was not even half full. Howie Parish was the only student I recognized, so I bounced over to sit by him.

The class bell rang. Professor Thomas Alfred DuLaney stood beside his desk in a vested dark suit, brightened by a gold watch chain swinging over his midriff.

After calling the roll he put down his class book and surveyed us in puzzlement. "I can't understand why more students didn't sign up for this class. Two world wars have started in Europe in this century. I'd think that they'd want to know more about Europe so we could prevent a future conflict. But I suppose," he sighed, "that the pundit spoke for many people when he said, 'All that we ever learn from history is that we never learn from history.' "

Our little sawed-off professor was up and running. He contrasted different theories of history. "Do men make history, or does history make men? Do generals and presidents and kings do what they are forced to do by the economic and social situations of their time? Or, is history part of a divine plan with people playing out their roles?"

Howie's hand shot up. He was interested in the theories of history, but he wanted Mr. DuLaney's prediction on when the Allies were going to invade France.

Mr. DuLaney reached in his inside coat pocket and produced a paper. "Well, it happens that President Hull has just issued a statement on the upcoming invasion. He doesn't think the current differences between the Supreme Allied Commander, General Eisenhower and Prime Minister Churchill, are the reason for the delay. Mr. Hull thinks they may be disagreeing over some military tactics, perhaps about supply problems."

"But has a date been set?" Howie persisted.

Mr. DuLaney fished another paper from his pocket. "The Allied Headquarters in England sent this through military channels. It says an actual date has been set, but that date is not specified. I guess we'll know when we know."

Mr. DuLaney pushed the papers back into his suit coat pocket and returned to the subject at hand. During the next 12 weeks, he promised to guide us through the building of European nations from feudalism to modern times. Just before dismissal, he gave us a reading assignment in the textbook. He also said something about paying attention to footnotes which I didn't fully catch.

Dinner didn't come too soon. Josh was back at the barn cleaning stables. I sat with Junior and C.B. from Judy. Three tables ahead of us Jeri Lynn Anderson reigned over Howie Parish and two other male scholars whose names I didn't yet know. Most girls didn't have even one college boy at their table, which compared to Jeri Lynn, didn't seem quite fair.

I was lingering over Joe Sidney's peach cobbler special when the first company of naval cadets poured into the dining hall. One cadet bumped a big Tech boy, Rags Denney. Rags shoved back. Another cadet threw a punch and missed his target. Cadets began chanting at the collegiate males, "Draft dodgers! Draft dodgers! Four F! Four F!"

Food services manager Paul Fiser, a fat cigar spouting from his lips, came rushing into the melee, hollering, "Here, here! Break it up!"

A serving woman called President Hull in his office. He came running. With more help from the cadet commander, a riot was squelched.

Mr. Fiser shouted over the speaker system, "When you finish your meal, please leave." He had to help a few male students out the door.

Junior and C.B. had already left for their one o'clock class. With an hour before Arkansas History, I decided to look around the campus some more. Strolling along the sidewalk that ran parallel with the west side of Ole Main, I spotted a shiny Chevy convertible easing down El Paso Avenue. A big carrot-topped fellow with a pumpkin grin beamed proudly from behind the wheel. Three girls were jammed in front with Ole Carrot Top. Five females, including Marie and Emma, were squished in the back seat.

I'd seen the driver at registration the day before, but didn't know his name.

Marie waved to me. "C'mon, 'Fesser. Jump in," she squealed. Never having ridden in a convertible before, I ran toward them. Ole Carrot Top took one look at me and sped away laughing.

I hoofed back to Ole Main and checked my watch. Twenty minutes until Arkansas History, my last class, after which I planned on buying my textbooks at the Techionery. My last class on Friday, phys. ed., came at four p.m. Then Saturday morning, hip, hip, hooray, I'd be going home for the weekend.

I was twisting about on the entry walk to Ole Main, seeing what I could see, when Carrot Top wheeled into a parking slot. The girls piled out. Marie strolled over to me, freckles popping with amusement. "Couldn't catch us, huh?"

"Nope," I conceded. "Who's the guy?"

"George Maloney. We all call him Georgie. Ain't he cute?"

"Aw, you only think that 'cause he's got a convertible. I bet he's either 4F, or his daddy knows somebody on his draft board."

Marie ignored my gibe. "His daddy has a Chevy dealership in Little Rock. Georgie can have any car he wants."

"My daddy has a coon dog dealership in Mount

Judy and drives a Model A truck. I can have any dog I want."

"That's funny, 'Fesser." She eyed me up and down. "You'd look cute in them overalls, drivin' a convertible down El Paso Avenue."

A trace of envy crossed my face. "You know I ain't old enuff to drive, even if I had a convertible."

She shifted her shoulders. "Well, when you get a car and get old enough to drive it, you can take me out."

"By then I hope to be long gone from Tech." I looked at my watch. "I gotta get to Mr. DuLaney's Arkansas History."

"Me too," she said. "Let's go."

It didn't matter that Marie towered over me. I skipped along beside her, through the double doors, and up the stairs to the second floor classroom where we made a grand entrance together.

Mr. DuLaney was checking his notes — "to see if the pages are in numerical order," he said in a tone of preciseness.

Josh came bumbling in and collapsed into a chair at the back. The prof looked at him with a sly grin. "Why did you choose this class, Mr. Brown?"

Josh's honest reply came quick. "Cuz it's required."

"Very good, Mr. Brown. I g-guess that's reason enough.

"Now let's see how much you good people know about your state. To start with, who can give us the origin of the name 'Arkansas'?"

I couldn't hold back: "It came from the Bible."

Mr. DuLaney's face showed puzzlement. "From

the Bible," he repeated. "Will our young Bible scholar in overalls please give us the chapter and verse."

"I ain't no Bible scholar. Somewhar' in Genesis it says, 'Noah looked into the ark and saw.' "

Marie tee-heed. Josh almost fell off his chair.

Mr. DuLaney kept a straight face. "That wasn't quite what I had in mind."

Ole teacher pleaser Howie Parish piped up, "Our textbook, professor, says the word Arkansas came from the Algonquin or Quapaw Indians."

Of course, Mr. DuLaney had to compliment Howie, just as Miss Massie had in her morning class. This time, Josh didn't keep his scowl to himself.

Mr. DuLaney continued his overview, answering his own questions. "Who was the first white man to see Arkansas? De Soto.

"How did Arkansas become a territory of the United States? It came with the Louisiana Purchase.

"Where was the first school established in Arkansas Territory? Dwight Mission, in 1820," Mr. DuLaney told us. "The site is just a few miles from here. The school was started by Reverend Cephas Washburn for Cherokee Indian children whose families came here on the terrible Trail of Tears."

Mr. Dulaney jumped forward a few score years. "What famous American general was born in Arkansas? Douglas MacArthur, born in Little Rock, January 26, 1880. His father, Arthur MacArthur, was a famous general in the Civil War and won the Congressional Medal of Honor."

Mr. DuLaney noticed a funny looking smirk edge across my face. "Mr. Hefley is dying to say something. Go ahead."

"Isn't there a song named for Ole MacArthur?"

Mr. DuLaney actually took me seriously. "You tell us, Mr. Hefley."

"Ole MacArthur had a farm, eee yi, eee yi, oh and on that farm — "

Mr. Dulaney cut me off at the pass. "Your humor may be appreciated at the grade school level, but not at college, Mr. Hefley. Now may I continue?"

My face burned. Marie tittered. No one else emitted a sound. If I had been sitting on a front row, I think I would have crawled out the door.

After what seemed an eternity, the bell rang. Mr. DuLaney held out his hand. "One minute, please. Remember your reading assignment in the textbook. And I'd also advise you to become familiar with the references listed in the footnotes. You never can tell what might turn up on a test."

Mr. DuLaney then dismissed us. Marie was the only one who spoke to me as we left the room. "I don't think Mr. DuLaney has a very good sense of humor," she said.

My spirits lifted and I offered to walk her back to Caraway Hall, the women's dorm, where I presumed she was living. "The WACs are camped in Caraway," she noted. "Civilian girls are bunking in the Fine Arts Building and anywhere else they can find a room for us. Right now I'm goin' to the Techionery to get my textbooks."

"Ain't that somethin'," I remarked. "I'm headed over that way, too. C'mon, I'll give you a ride on my bike."

Marie actually jumped on behind me. We got lots

of laughs, with all 110 pounds of little me pedalling furiously to keep the bike from twisting and falling over. Half way there, she slid off and bruised her knee. The amused glances of students walking in the area didn't help my pride one bit. When I invited her back on, she said, "No thanks, 'Fesser, I can make it the rest of the way by myself."

I got there first and was paying for my books when she arrived. I offered to wait and carry her books back to where she was staying. She didn't even say "no thanks."

Figuring that I'd better leave well enough alone, I jumped on my bike and headed for the house on L Street. By the time I got there, I was too tired to play with Lem and his neighborhood friend. Certainly too tired to pull on my Sears and Roebuck tweed suit and bike back to the campus for the formal freshman reception and dance that evening. My coming out in Tech society would have to wait.

I picked up Miss Massie's Composition and Rhetoric book and fell across the bed. The words blurred before my eyes. Szzzzzzzz.

It had been a long day.

Chapter 6

"Making Points With Professor DuLaney"

Aunt Jane was planting sweet corn in her garden behind the house and didn't check on me until time came to fix supper. She heard me snoring and knocked lightly.

"James Carl, don't you have some studying to do?"

I rubbed my eyes. "Oh, yeah. I must have dozed off looking at my English book."

Mama's cousin cracked my door. "Oh, I see you changed back to overalls. Did you hang up your school pants?"

"Unhuh." I didn't tell her I'd worn overalls for my first day of classes.

Aunt Jane moved back into the kitchen. I picked up Miss Massie's book that I had dropped when falling asleep and tried to focus on pronouns.

"Sometimes a pronoun takes the place of another pronoun." Buzz, buzz. I swatted at a red wasp that had flown in through a hole in the window screen.

The book gave an example: "ONE of our dogs is missing. IT was last heard from over four hours ago. IT takes the place of ONE."

The wasp lit on the bed. I thumped IT dead with my book.

Then I remembered that English wouldn't meet again until Friday, two days in the future. Tomorrow — Thursday — I had only Arkansas History, a five-day-a-week class. English and European History could wait.

I checked the time on my pocket watch. Five-thirty. I headed for the living room and flipped on the Essex's Philco console.

"Jack Armstrong! Jack Armstrong! The All-American Boy." The radio swept me into another world. I was sprawled on the floor, ears tuned to the next serial, "Captain Midnight," when Aunt Jane called, "Supper time!"

The next morning Aunt June made sure I had my school pants on when I left the house. I biked to the Tech library and read a couple of chapters in *Arkansas History*. The explorations of Hernando DeSoto in the 1500s intrigued me. The book said he might have visited the Ozarks before returning to the Mississippi River where he died of fever. I was mulling that over when a big finger tapped the back of my head. I whirled to see a grinning Josh Brown. I hadn't noticed him working behind a shelf of books.

"Hey, let's go get some air," he proposed.

I slapped my *Arkansas History* shut and ambled outside with Josh. We talked about DeSoto's trips and speculated about whether he had found gold in

Arkansas. Josh didn't think he had. "There ain't no gold in this state. Ain't nuthin' in Arkansas but scrub oak and hard work."

"Hey, ya wanna go to Judy with me Saturday?" I invited. "Ride the Red Ball bus to Lurton and Daddy'll meet us there. We can go fishin' an' come back Sunday evenin'."

Josh frowned. "I gotta work at the college farm all day. 'Sides, I ain't got enuff money fer the bus ticket."

I pulled out my dollar watch. "We'd better be gettin' on over to Ole Main for Mr. DuLaney's class."

A chunky, cotton-headed fellow caught up with us. "I'm Jack Sampson. Ever'body calls me Whitey."

We introduced ourselves. "Ever'body knows you, James Carl," Whitey said. "You're the boy marvel. Imagine, going to college at 13. You'll have a Ph.D. before 20."

Josh spotted Mr. Tomlinson, the science teacher and farm supervisor, coming out of the Fine Arts Building with a tall, light-haired lady. "That's Miss Lela Jane Bryan, the home ec. teacher," Josh informed us. "I hear Mr. Tommy's sweet on her."

"Mr. Tommy?" I questioned.

"Thet's what ever'body calls Mr. Tomlinson," he informed us.

Mr. Tommy saw Josh and crooked a finger at him. Josh excused himself "to see whut mah boss wants."

Whitey strolled on with me. "I'm an officer in the BSU," he noted.

"What's that?" I wondered. "Some kind of club?"

"Baptist Student Union. I'd like to invite you to our BSU social, at seven in the evening, a week from Friday, in the dining hall."

"I don't belong to no church."

"You're not a Christian?"

"Nah. I ain't never been baptized. Hain't no Baptists in my family, anyway. Them that have been baptized, belong to other churches."

Josh caught up with us at the door of Mr. DuLaney's classroom. Whitey grabbed me. "You don't have to be a church member to attend our social. We'd also be glad to have you in our Bible study group."

I didn't give Whitey any encouragement. "I'm takin' five subjects. I don't have time for another one."

"Well, you'll be welcome to our BSU events whenever you can come."

Mr. DuLaney's desk sat to the right, just inside the door. Howie Parish was bending his ear. Remembering my Wednesday goof, I slipped by without saying anything.

The bell rang. Mr. DuLaney called the roll, then got down to business. "Yesterday, class, we pointed out some of the high marks in Arkansas history. Today, we'll start with the first inhabitants of this great state — the Indians."

My spirits picked up. One of the few books I had read at Judy High School was about Indians. When he began asking questions, I was ready.

"Who were the first human inhabitants?"

I lifted my hand and got permission to speak. "The Bluff Dwellers. They lived in bluff houses and caves. We know they w'ar hyar, but we don't know whut happened to 'um."

The way I rattled on, you'd have thought I was Mr. DuLaney's star pupil. Finally, though, he said, "Mr. Hefley, let's give somebody else a chance to show their learning."

Howie slapped me on my skinny shoulder as we left class. "This was your day to shine, Hefley. Keep that up and you'll get a triple-A grade."

I couldn't get used to the guys calling each other by their last names. If you called out "Hefley" in Judy half the town would have answered.

I pedalled back to Aunt Jane's house feeling all grown up.

The next day was another story. That Friday was March 17th, Saint Patrick's Day. What a rough day. I mean, rough. The only thing that kept me going was the anticipation of going home for the weekend.

The day started off badly. Aunt June caught me leaving the house in my overalls and ordered me back to change into pants.

"You're not my mama," I screeched.

"Your mother left you in my charge. If you're going to college, you are wearing pants, not overalls."

I grudgingly trudged back and changed.

It had rained buckets the night before and I pedalled right into a mud hole. The bike slipped to one side and I slid off into the mud. It was a miracle that my books stayed dry.

Then Miss Massie gave an awful pop test on the

usages of the eight parts of speech. You'd have had to memorize the entire first chapter to have made a decent grade. Worse, she caught a couple of girls mouthing answers to each other. "You two just scored a big zero on this quiz," she informed them.

Miss Massie's eagle eyes swept over the room. "Pass your papers to the front. They'll be returned on Monday."

Only typing was a breeze. I loved every minute and lingered behind to tell Mrs. Clark, "You're my favorite perfesser."

In European History, Mr. DuLaney lost me somewhere between the Norman attack on England and the crowning of King Henry the Fourth.

Later, in Arkansas History, Mr. DuLaney called Marie and me down for whispering. "You're not third graders," he reminded us. "You're in college now where in my classes you will be graded on respect and deportment." He also scolded me for my muddy pants, reminding the entire class that many alumni and other visitors were on the campus to celebrate Engineers Day.

It seems the Engineers were allowed to rule the campus on St. Pat's Day when they initiated new pledges into their club. When I was going to the dining hall for dinner there stood that ole showoff Georgie Maloney twirling a wooden cogwheel around his neck. Why the Engineers had chosen him as one of their "fish" pledges, I couldn't figure, but he seemed really proud of wearing their symbol.

Howie, who had already been initiated as an Engineers, shouted at Georgie, "Go roll in the grass, fish."

Georgie saluted. "Your humble servant obeys your command." Georgie dropped his books, fell to the wet ground, and rolled like a ball.

"Very good, Maloney," Howie declared. "Now sing me a song. Loud!"

Georgie lifted his croaky voice.

> We are the engineers,
> We're always on the spot,
> When there's work to do,
> We really do a lot.
> When Agris come nearby,
> All of us may yell,
> 'Agris, Agris,
> Why don't you go to, well?' "

Howie threw me a grin, "Let's go get some food in our bellies." As we entered the dining hall, I heard another Engineer's voice addressing Georgie. "Fish, come take my dirty dishes away."

When I left the dining hall, leaving Howie engaged in a drippy conversation with Jeri Lynn, a new "fish" was squatting on the steps. This one was emptying a bucket of water into another bucket with a thimble. Nearby, three more fish pledges sat on the sidewalk, yelling, "I'm a fool! I'm a fool!"

All that day, Engineers kept button-holing people and telling put-down jokes about their arch rivals, the Agris. They'd ask questions like, "Did you hear about the little Agri who…

"Cut off his arms so he could wear sleeveless sweaters?"

"Jumped through the screen and strained

himself?"

"Took a bicycle to bed with him so he wouldn't walk in his sleep."

"Sat at a street intersection with two slices of bread, waiting for the traffic jam?"

"Put the clock under his bed at night so he could get up on time?"

"Took cream and sugar to the picture show because he'd heard there was goin' to be a serial?"

"Called his girl 'Postscript,' because her name was Adaline?"

That evening President Hull was going to crown Richard Bryan as St. Patrick. Then Richard would crown Miss Judy Jones as the Engineers' queen. After that the nine pledges would kiss the "blarney stone" and be knighted Engineers by St. Patrick. The Engineers' ball would follow in the Armory.

None of it appealed to me. Playing marbles and catching crawdads was more my idea of a fun time.

I tried to ignore all the goings on and reported with the rest of the boys to the football field. It was our first phys. ed. class of the quarter. Mr. Fiser, our stocky instructor, stood at the gate, puffing on a smelly stogie, holding a roll book, checking our names off as we came galloping through.

A squad of Naval Air Cadets were busy on the east side of the field, climbing a 20-foot-high net, then swinging down on ropes.

I was running toward the net to show off my climbing skills, when Mr. Fiser hollered, "Hefley, get back here.

"Stay away from the cadets," he ordered all of us.

"That's their end of the field." He waved a hairy arm. "Over to the right here is ours." He looked at me and smiled. "Sorry, Hefley, we don't have a net for monkeys.

"Now, everybody sit down on the grass in front of me and listen for a few minutes," he commanded.

"There are three parts to every one of us, mind, body and soul. Or to put it another way, the physical, mental and spiritual. You exercise the spiritual when you pray and go to church on Sunday. Your mind gets a workout in classes." He cast us a sly grin. "Miss Massie, I understand, is pretty good with exercises for the mind.

"And I am the one whose job it is to see that you give your body some attention.

"As the food director, I'm responsible for providing a healthy, balanced diet. As your phys. ed. coach, my job is to get you in a good program of exercise.

"Okay? Am I making myself clear?"

"Yeah, coach!" we yelled.

"Now I'm gonna go light on you today. We'll do about ten minutes of calisthenics, run around the track a few times, and end up with a little football."

He sent us over to a dressing room under the stands to change into shorts. Neither Josh nor I had brought any. "I'll let you boys work out in your school clothes this time," Mr. Fiser conceded, "but next Friday you had better have the proper dress."

I didn't know about Josh, and I didn't dare tell Mr. Fiser that I had never worn a pair of shorts in my life. Nor did I want to disclose in the dressing room that I wasn't wearing any underwear.

The instructor lined us all up across the west end of the field. "First, we're gonna do some pushups. Like this." He fell down on all fours. "Back and legs straight. Now, down and up, one; down and up, two. Can you see me? Okay, let's do ten together."

My arms were not much bigger than a broom stick. The third time down I flopped. Josh, who had arms nearly the size of a stove pipe, stayed with the count.

I skipped a couple, tried again, flopped. A moan sounded to the right of Josh. I looked over and saw Ole Carrot Top, Georgie Maloney lying flat on his face in the grass.

Coach Fiser's "Ten!" was the best word I'd heard all day. His face, Howie Parish's, and Josh Brown's didn't look the least bit flushed. Mine and Ole Carrot Top's were melting.

"Now we're gonna do a dozen sit-ups. Like this," Coach Fiser demonstrated smoothly.

The sit-ups weren't so bad. I did eight before falling back on my rear. Howie and Josh were still going. Georgie was twisting in pain.

Coach Fiser led us through a couple of other routines, then turned us loose for four laps around the track. Georgie did only two laps and plopped down, chest heaving. I ran like a rabbit, dashing ahead of Howie, Josh and most of the rest.

The coach looked on approvingly. "Way to go, Hefley! I knew you could do something. Way to go!"

Next, Coach divided us into two squads for a game of football. I had never seen a football game of

any variety in my life. In Judy, if someone said
"pigskin," you'd have thought they were referring to
a porker's hide.

He called for Howie Parish to stand in front of
him. "In phys. ed. football," Coach said, "the ball
carrier is down when an opponent touches him. The
tackles stand upright and shove the players facing
them. Like this." He heaved his body, catching
Howie off guard, pushing him over.

"Let's go at it again, Parish," our instructor said.

Even though Howie was ready this time, Coach
pushed him to the ground like a feather. Howie was
impressed. All of us were.

"Okay," Coach directed. "let's have two boys
volunteer as captains. How about you, Parish, and
you, Sampson."

Coach pulled out a coin. Howie called "heads."
The coin came up tails, so Whitey, the Baptist boy,
picked first.

For some funny reason, I came in next to the last
pick, Georgie Maloney. That's how we came to face
each other on the line.

Ole Carrot Top weighed more than twice as much
as I did. Nevertheless, when the play was called, I
plowed into him, bumping my little round head into
his soft belly.

"Ooomph! Owww!" he groaned and fell over.

On the next play I slammed him down again.
"Football is fun," I told a grimacing Georgie.

From then on, Georgie collapsed with moans
every time I hit him. It got to where when a play was
called, the other boys would watch me block Georgie

before doing their own thing. I almost felt sorry for him. He was such a big ole puff ball. Still, he just moaned and didn't get mad.

Coach didn't dismiss us until five minutes to six. My face was streaked with sweat. My pants looked as if they'd been dragged down a muddy ditch. I winced when Josh slapped me on the shoulder. "You shore took care of ole Georgie," he said. "You shore put 'em in the dirt."

Even with my aches and pains, I felt good all over. *Tomorrow when I can go jump in the Rock Hole,* I thought, *everything will be perfect.*

Chapter 7

"A Quick Trip Home"

T hat you, James Carl?" Aunt Jane called as I dragged my book bag across the porch.

"Yes'um, and I'm wore to a frazzle."

Her motherly instinct took over when she saw my clothes. "What happened?" she gasped.

I told her about falling into the mudhole and not having shorts for phys. ed. class, noting that I had forgotten to wear Uncle George's underwear.

"I'll pin you up another pair," she promised. "And if you don't start wearing them, I'll start checking you in the mornings."

Heavy footsteps sounded on the porch. "There's George now. I'll hurry and finish supper. I know you both are starved."

After supper Uncle George and I moved into the living room to hear the nightly report of the staccato newscaster, Walter Winchell.

> Good evening, Mr. and Mrs. North America and all the ships at sea.

"Turn it up so I can hear," Aunt Jane hollered from the kitchen where she was washing the dishes.

…There's good news from the Pacific war theater. A dispatch just in reports that American troops have captured the last of the Admiralty Islands. If you know your geography, the Admiralties are just north of New Guinea…

…Meanwhile, across the Atlantic in Europe, the rumor mill is humming over speculation of when the beaches of France will be filled with Allied soldiers…. For the champions of freedom, that will not come a minute too soon….

…Now for some very good news in the science of medicine. In a few days it will be announced that the wonder drug penicillin will be available to civilians. For people suffering from many previously incurable diseases, including deadly infections, the penicillin cure will not come a minute too soon. Here's a hearty salute to Dr. Alexander Fleming, the discoverer, the father of penicillin….

And now a message from our sponsor…

Uncle George stood up and stretched. Aunt Jane came in and saw me nodding. "James Carl, go take your shower and get in bed. You've got to be up early tomorrow to catch the Red Ball bus."

She didn't have to beg me. I fell asleep almost instantly. The next thing I felt was Aunt Jane shaking my shoulder, saying it was time to rise and shine. I donned a clean pair of overalls and wolfed down a bowl of oatmeal with Uncle George. Ten minutes later he dropped me at the bus station on Main Street in Russellville.

I was at the counter getting my ticket when a whiff of perfume sailed by my nose. I felt a tap on my shoulder. Jeri Lynn Anderson and Howie Parish.

"Howie brought me down to catch the Red Ball for a visit home," Jeri Lynn chirped. "Looks like we'll be ridin' together, James Carl."

That was all right with me.

The Red Ball pulled in a few minutes later and parked beside a big Greyhound. The little bus was no more than a small van, with a red, goose-egg sized tin ball, hanging above the windshield. Mama's Uncle George Sutton stepped out. "Hi there, Jeri Lynn." He looked at me. "And you're James Carl, ain'tcha, Fred and Hester's son. Reckon you and Jeri Lynn must be goin' home fer the weekend."

Clem and Joel, two other Tech boys who knew Jeri Lynn, sat in back of us. They were headed for Deer, about 15 miles north of Lurton, where Daddy would meet me. I kept trying to talk to Jeri Lynn. They kept interrupting.

"Joined any clubs?" Jeri Lynn asked me.

"Me and Clem are Agris," Joel answered.

Jeri Lynn ignored him. "I've joined the Wesley Foundation," she told me. "That's the Methodist Club. They do a lot of fun things."

"Whitey Sampson asked me to come to a Baptist Student Union dinner. I told him I wasn't a Baptist, or a member of any church."

"I don't belong to any church, either," Jeri Lynn said. "The Wesley kids said that didn't matter."

"Well, I ain't gonna join a Baptist club where I don't belong."

We moved on to Miss Massie. "She really thinks she's somethin'," Clem commented from behind. "If her class warn't required, I shore wouldn't be in thar."

We chewed on Miss Massie through Bull Frog Valley and picked up on Mr. DuLaney when the Red Ball crossed Booger Holler. At the top of the mountain, Joel brought Mr. Tommy into the act. "Ever'body loves that ole man. He's a widower, ya know. Sweet on Miss Lela Jane Bryan, I hear."

Clem was in my phys. ed. class. He slapped me on the shoulder. "I most 'bout busted a gut laughin' watchin' you slam into Georgie Maloney. He's a real puff ball. The girls only like him because he's got a Chevy convertible," Clem added.

"Yeh," Joel agreed. "But Coach Fiser will make a man out of him."

"Whata ya know about ole Fiser?" I asked Clem.

"He piled up quite a record in sports. I saw an old *Arka-Tech* paper that said he made all state in football and baseball while in high school, then lettered four years in baseball and football at Arkansas College. He also pitched in minor-league baseball, 'till a sore arm took him out."

"Next stop, Anderson's Store," Uncle George called.

Jeri Lynn gathered up her things and was ready when the bus stopped. "See you fellers tomorrow evenin' on the way back," she called.

Twenty minutes later we pulled into Lurton. I stepped into Irving and Ruby Sutton's store. Fifteen more miles to Judy. A half hour's ride in Daddy's Model A. So I thought. Irving hadn't seen "hide nar hair" of Daddy.

"But I wrote him to meet me here when the Red

Ball came."

"Maybe he had a flat," Irving suggested. "Give him a little more time."

The Red Ball left. I was beginning to feel abandoned. "You know anybody around here who's driving to Judy today?" I asked Ruby.

She didn't.

An hour later I gave up and started walking down dusty Hwy 123. Two miles out, I had to make a decision at the junction with the Cave Creek road. Both roads led to Judy. The Cave Creek route was further, but Daddy was unpredictable. He could have decided to go squirrel hunting on Cave Creek. I took a chance and stayed on 123.

A half mile farther on I passed through the old town of Carver. All that remained was a pond, a graveyard, and the Haynes' house. I saw the oldest Haynes girl, Colleen, lolling on the porch. "Seen my daddy comin' this way?" She hadn't.

Nine more long miles of walking down the tree-shaded road, I came to the Judy forest tower and sat down to rest. Putt, putt, putt! I scrambled to my feet. Yo, yo, yo! Hound dogs barking. Daddy's Model A clattered into view.

I ran to meet him. Daddy jolted to a stop, rubbing his eyes in surprise.

"Daddy, you were supposed to meet the Red Ball fer me. Didn't you get my letter yesterday that I was comin' home fer the weekend?"

He shook his head. "South mail didn't run yesterday, son. Ole Doyne must have been sick. Didja walk all the way from Lurton?"

I bobbed my sweaty little noggin straight up and down.

"I was goin' squirrel huntin up hyar around the tower. Reckon I'd better git you home now. Yer mama gits yer letter today with me gone, she'll be powerful upset."

The Model A carried us down the mountain curves to Judy. Mama hugged me as if she hadn't seen me in a year. "I got your letter after yer daddy left. Came in today's mail."

It was Saturday and there was a crowd in town. Cousins Billy Buck and Goober and others swarmed around me. I saw Monk and his dog Danny Boy running toward Daddy's garage on the other side of the street.

"Yip! Yip!" A flash of brown fur just about knocked me down. Ole Shep! I hugged him tight.

Mama asked the question that was on everybody's tongue: "Did you quit college?"

"No, Mama, I jist wanted to come home and see ever'body and go fishin'."

Ole Shep jumped up on my leg and barked. "See, Mama, how much he missed me?"

A customer called from the front door of the store. "Hester, kin ya come?" Mama gave me another hug, saying, "We'll talk more later."

Monk came back from Daddy's garage with a coffee can and two reels. "Let's go ketch some horny-heads at the Rock Hole."

I forgot my tiredness. Billy Buck and Goober allowed that they would go too. The four of us skipped down Mill Hill and crossed to Grover

Greenhaw's barn lot. Monk grabbed a hoe and started turning over cow piles. In minutes, we had a can full of squirming, fat red worms.

From there we headed straight for the Rock Hole. We caught three stringersful of the little red-bumped horny-head fish that swim up Ozark creeks to spawn in the spring. Then we peeled off our clothes and jumped in the cold March water. Ole Shep and Danny Boy came splashing in with us.

That evening it was cool enough to have a fire in our big living room wood stove. After supper we sat around gabbing, Mama and Daddy and their six kids, with a boodle of cousins, aunts and uncles, and other visitors looking on. The Grand Ole Opry played in the background.

They wanted to know about my classes, and which one did I like best. I told them typing.

"What 'er ya studyin' to be?" Cousin Gussie asked.

"I'm majorin' in business."

Gussie threw her glance to Mama. "Hester, I tho't you told me that James Carl was goin' to be a doctor."

"Well, yes I did, Gussie," Mama said. "He can always change his mind."

I knew right then that Mama hadn't lost hope that her boy would take Doc Sutton's place in the family.

A shriek came from the radio. "Howdeee, I'm jist so glad to be hyar."

Minnie Pearl. We listened while she told about her current "feller."

Roy Acuff sang "The Wabash Cannon Ball." Then the Duke of Paducah did his thing, ending, as he always did, "Ah'm headin' fer the wagon, boys. These shoes air killin' me."

Uncle Willie Pink allowed it was time for him to hit the hay. People began trickling out, until only our family was left. Mama noticed me nodding and hustled me upstairs to bed.

My eyes popped open the next morning to welcome the bright sunshine streaming through the side window. I lay there luxuriating and listening to the first robins of spring.

Mama's voice rang through the house. "James Carl, Howard Jean, Louise and Loucille, Jimmie and Freddie, come to breakfast." Then I heard her walking to the back porch. "Fred, come on and eat. Your hound dogs can wait."

We gathered around the table, Daddy coming last as usual. We dove in, with Mama circling the table to pour syrup on everyone's fluffy pancakes.

"Fred, don't forget," Mama reminded when Daddy finished. "You and James Carl need to leave right after 12 o'clock for him to catch the Red Ball back to Tech.

With no thought of helping Mama with the dishes, I passed my dirty plate to her and ambled outside and up the street to the cafe. Uncle Bill Hefley had his big black Bible out and was debating the merits of baptism with muscular Raleigh Sexton. After awhile, Uncle Bill checked his pocket watch and announced that it was time for Sunday school.

"Any of you boys comin' with me? How about you, James Carl?" I shook my head. A couple of Uncle Bill's grandsons fell in step behind him, leaving the rest of us to our Sunday morning leisure.

The sun climbed higher. I drowsed on the cafe porch, petted ole Shep, shot marbles, told exaggerated stories about Miss Massie. Around 11, I got bored and began checking my watch.

I saw Mama come out of the store and hand Daddy a paper poke and two bottles of pop. Mama hollered at me to come and give her a goodbye hug. Daddy pitched a hound dog in the back of his Model A. I squeezed Mama, waved to my four little sisters — brother Monk had already gone to the creek — and climbed in the truck cab.

We started up the mountain. "I'm goin' squirrel huntin' on the way back from takin' you," Daddy said as he shifted into low. "Yer Mama put sandwiches fer us in that poke. Eat 'um 'fore we git to Lurton."

Daddy stopped to sic the dog after a possum that ran across the road. It dashed back toward the truck. Boom! One less possum. I picked it up and threw it in the back of the truck.

The Red Ball was waiting for me when we got to Lurton. Daddy explained our delay to Uncle George Sutton who just said, "Come on and get in, James Carl. Jeri Lynn will be waitin' fer us at her daddy's store."

I climbed in behind Clem and Joel. At Anderson's Store, they invited Jeri Lynn to sit between them. She pushed in beside me and whispered in my ear, "They're a little too fresh for me."

Except for a flat in Booger Holler, we made good

time and rolled into the Russellville bus station a little after three o'clock.

Howie Parish was there to meet Jeri Lynn and offered to take me to the Essex's. "Uncle George will be down to get me," I assured them.

The Greyhound agent saw me waiting and handed over a thin telephone directory. I found the name, George Essex. I began fumbling around with a telephone — I had never used one before. The agent finally had to show me how to call and give the operator the three digit number.

"I'm sorry, but your party does not answer," the operator said mechanically. "Call back later."

As I was putting down the phone, a familiar female voice hollered from the door. "Sorry, we're late, James Carl."

Aunt Jane sniffed me over good when I got in the truck. "You smell like a possum. When we get home, in the shower you go. Then you work on your lessons for tomorrow."

Chapter 8

"On a Wing and a Prayer"

The highlight of my second week at Tech was when the article about me appeared on the front page of the *Arka-Tech*. It was headlined:

13-YEAR-OLD TECH STUDENT READS LONGFELLOW AND "JITTERS"

That reporter had made me out to be a kind of literary scholar, which I was not. The article claimed: "He frequently coasts through the material of such writers as Washington Irving, Longfellow, and Bret Harte."

Well, I did know two lines from Longfellow:

> Listen my children and you shall hear
> Of the midnight ride of Paul Revere.

Then it talked about me liking "Jitters." Actually I had read that comic strip for the first time the morning of the interview.

Everyone on campus read the article and I basked in the attention. At least until Miss Massie had some cryptic comments to make about me being a "literary scholar."

After that my days at Tech that spring term fell into a routine. Got up at 6:30 and stood under the shower. It would be years before I'd need to shave.

Seven o'clock breakfast, then a dress inspection by Aunt Jane who declared that I must "never ever, no never" wear overalls to class again. Seven forty and I was on my bike, heading for Miss Massie's eight o'clock Composition and Rhetoric class.

Except for Miss Massie's Monday, Wednesday, Friday class, I was surviving (though barely in Mr. DuLaney's history classes) my other subjects.

That old maid was on my case at every opportunity. "Mr. Hefley, 'ain't' is out of bounds in respectable conversation. If you don't stop using that word, I may have to exercise my faculty privileges and throw you out of this class.

"'Done gone' is a mark of ignorance. 'Had went' is worse."

" 'Went a fer piece' is not how educated ladies and gentlemen talk. Traveled a long distance is acceptable."

At the third weekly assembly of the term, Dr. Hull announced there would be a college wiener roast at Skyline Park on top of Mt. Nebo. Miss Massie, Mr. Tommy, and Miss Lela Jane Bryan, the home ec. teacher, would chaperon.

"A bus load of naval air cadets will be going with us," the president said. "You'll have a great time with them." Remembering the fracas the cadets and the college boys had had in the dining hall I wasn't so sure.

Josh and I boarded the bus early. "When Emma Harper gets on," he said, "I'm gonna ask her to set with me and be mah date. You kin ask Marie Singleton."

"Naw, I ain't datin' no girl." Miss Massie cast her

eyes toward me. I winced. I didn't dare say what I was thinking: *That woman must have ears in the back of her head.*

Emma came and sat down beside a grinning Josh. Marie plopped down beside me without me asking. Part way up Nebo I spotted a familiar figure plowing in a field on my side of the bus. It was the farmer that had sold Daddy a load of watermelons the previous fall. I stuck my head and upper torso out the window and hollered, "I'm Fred Hefley's boy. Save me a big'un when they get ripe." He threw a big paw in the air to assure me that he would.

The bus jolted to a stop. The driver had seen me in his rear view mirror. He leaned over and spoke to Miss Massie. She stalked back to where Marie and I were sitting.

"Mr. Hefley, the college is responsible for your safety. If you do that again, I'll see that you walk back to the campus."

I muttered my sorries, not daring to look her in the eye, while Marie sat beside me as stiff as a board. Finally, Miss Massie moved back to her front seat. The bus continued up the mountain.

At the top, the driver parked behind the cadet bus. Joe Sidney, the cook, and a couple of Tech student workers were already on the grounds, stoking two big fires. The chilly air on top of the mountain brought shivers. Neither Marie nor I had brought a coat.

A big, rusty-haired cadet came walking toward Marie. They'd sat together for a meal once in the dining hall. She batted her eyes and greeted him with a "hi there." For the rest of the evening they sat making eyes at each other. I might as well have not existed.

Still, it turned out to be a fun evening. We played leap frog and engaged in grass fights. I stuffed a handful of clover down a girl's back. She swung at me. I ducked and fell backwards, landing in the arms of Miss Lela Jane Bryan, the home ec. teacher, who was Mr. Tommy's date for the evening. Mr. Tommy reached over and lifted me to my feet. I pulled up another sprig of clover and pitched it at Marie who was whispering in her cadet's ear.

The cadet commander introduced a boy from Ohio who got everybody's attention with slick card tricks. He pulled an ace from Mr. Tommy's right ear and a queen from Miss Massie's hairdo. Miss Massie actually laughed.

The dining hall crew served hot dogs, salad, baked beans and ice cream. They passed out wire hangers for us to string the dogs on. Josh wormed four along his wire, two for himself and two for Emma. "Why don't you put some dogs on for Marie?" he asked me.

I pointed across to the other fire where Marie was leaning against her cadet. "She's done jined the Navy."

Josh playfully swung a smoking dog at me. "If you'd asked her fer a date as ah told yuh too, she'd be leanin' on you now."

I stuck out my tongue at big Josh. "She'd a done knocked me over if she'd been leanin' on me." I glanced around fearfully at Miss Massie roasting a dog on the other side of the fire. If she'd heard me, she didn't let on.

Marie rode back to the campus on the cadet bus.

That wasn't so bad since another girl came and sat with me. This one didn't smack gum like Marie.

The next week Marie's cadet was transferred to the West coast. Marie cried when she told of their sad farewells. "I just know he's goin' into combat. He'll probably be killed."

Friday I phoned Aunt Jane to tell her I would be late coming home. After phys. ed. Josh, Emma, Marie and I were sitting in the Techionery, sipping milk shakes and listening to the juke box. When Ole Blue Eyes started with, "I'll Never Smile Again," Marie started boohooing all over the place.

A little while later Marie noticed me eying the clock on the wall. "It ain't late, Fesser. Whatcha so fidgety for."

"I, uh, got somethin' to do at my aunt's house."

Josh laughed. "Ya got a curfew? Nine o'clock's purty early for Friday night."

I eased out of the booth without explaining that Aunt Jane and Uncle George went to bed at nine. Aunt Jane was looking out the window when I wheeled up. "You're exactly one minute late, young man. Come and get ready for bed. You can stay up late tomorrow night and listen to the Grand Ole Opry."

Ten minutes later Aunt Jane turned out the lights.

Next morning after breakfast, I pulled my rod and reel from the closet which I'd brought back from my trip home. "You goin' fishin' in the little creek?" Uncle George asked. "Hain't nothin' but tadpoles and crawdads in there."

I flashed him a grin, shuffled out the door, and pulled a tin can from under the porch. I did go to the creek, but stayed only long enough to catch a can full of crawdads. Then I biked west, crossed the campus, and located Josh feeding cows at the Red Barn.

"Know how far to the Illinois Bayou?"

Josh waved a big paw. "Mr. Tommy says it's back behind them woods. You goin' by yerself? It ain't no little creek. You could slip in a sinkhole and drown."

Ignoring Josh's caution, I biked down a trail that got narrower and narrower, until I had to get off and push the bike to the bank of the big, muddy stream.

I hooked a crawdad on my line and cast out across the murky water. The current pushed the bait downstream and back toward the bank. Taking a few steps at a time, I kept casting without any luck. Finally I climbed out on a log that had fallen into the water, and dropped my bait straight down. Something began slowly pulling on my line. I knew what it was before I reeled in a little pancake sized snapping turtle.

I clipped off three feet of line and tied the turtle in my bike basket. By the time I tied on another hook, a cool, misty rain was falling. I picked up my can of crawdads and hurried back to seek shelter in the Red Barn.

Josh was pitching hay into a cow stall when I held up the turtle. "Miss Massie's gonna find this critter in her chair when she comes in for English class Monday morning."

"It might bite her," Josh warned.

"Good."

Josh put down his pitch fork and walked toward me. "'Fesser, you know that Miss Massie ain't one of mah favorite teachers. But she'll figger out who did it and flunk you fer shore."

"She's probably gonna flunk me anyway."

Josh eyed me critically. "'Fesser, I jist don't understand you, boy. When you registered fer classes, the teachers were makin' over how smart you were. Now you're provin' to them how dumb you are. Not to consider yer mama and daddy who are probably sacrificin' fer yuh to go to college.

"Let me give that little turtle to Mr. Tommy. He'll use it fer a zoology lesson. I'll tell him that you caught it."

I was beginning to feel ashamed of myself. I dropped the turtle in a slop bucket.

"Now git back to yer aunt and uncle's and study yer English lesson. Surprise Miss Massie and everybody else on Monday morning."

Trouble was I made the mistake of lying down to read the assigned chapter on phrases. I made it through prepositional and adjectival phrases, then fell asleep mumbling, "An adverbial phrase is a prepositional phrase that modifies an adverb, a verb...mmmmm, szzzzzz." The book dropped from my hands.

I woke up in time for supper, then stayed awake until midnight, listening to the Grand Ole Opry.

Sunday morning Aunt Jane and Uncle George got ready for church. Aunt Jane wanted me to go, but said, "I won't make you." So I didn't.

They were late coming home. Aunt Jane made sandwiches and soup, then sent me to my room to study Mr. DuLaney's European History. I began bogging down when the Lombards invaded Italy and destroyed the government of the Ostrogothic Kingdom. But I finished reading the assigned 28 pages, even if I couldn't have told the difference between the Goths and the Visigoths.

"I've finished," I announced to Aunt Jane. "I'm goin' over to the college gym and shoot goals."

I found Howie Parish there, all by his lonesome, slamming balls against the goal posts. He looked mad enough to choke a horse. Definitely not cool and collected, as he always appeared in class.

"Whatcha so mad about?" I asked.

"Jeri Lynn!" he snorted. "She's gone to a movie with a d____ cadet. We were supposed to go on a picnic together this afternoon."

"Forgit girls," I urged. "Let's play one on one to 20."

He calmed down and had a good time laughing at this silly little kid who was trying to beat the best ball player on campus. He gave me 10 points, then started dumping the ball in the basket. Final score 20-12. In Howie's favor, of course.

Around six o'clock I headed home for supper and a quick reading of a chapter on Arkansas as a territory. This was almost as confusing as Goths and Visigoths in European history. The United States got Arkansas as part of the big Louisiana Purchase. Then it belonged to Louisiana from 1804-12, then it was part of Missouri from 1812-19 when it became a separate territory. "Remember dates," Mr. DuLaney had said. "You might see them again on a test."

Sure enough, Mr. DuLaney gave a test on Monday, both in European and Arkansas History. He turned our papers back the next day. I got a D on each of the tests. Josh and Jeri Lynn each managed Cs, as did Emma and Marie. Howie, naturally, had As, with the notation, "Excellent work."

Emma was boiling. "I read and re-read every page of assigned readings in the textbooks. Half of the questions on the tests were about stuff that isn't in there."

A gloating smile spread across Howie's face. "What's so funny, smart alec?" Emma asked.

"Don't you remember him saying that we might get some questions on articles in books and journals listed in the footnotes of our textbooks. I read and made notes on every reference and it paid off."

"Now you're tellin' us," Emma said.

I spent Tuesday morning in the library, catching up on references footnoted in the two history texts. Just before the clock hit 12, I darted down the sidewalk to the dining hall. Josh, Emma and Marie waved me up to their place in line.

Coming out of the eatery later, I ran into a small crowd of students and faculty talking in low tones. "What happened?" I asked Whitey Sampson who was standing behind Mr. Tommy.

"June Talkington's missing in action. President Hull got word this morning."

I scratched my head. "Who's he?"

"Tell him, Mr. Tommy," Whitey requested.

"June was just the most popular fellow on campus when he was a student here. Charmed all the girls. His family is very well known in town. Parents are very supportive of the college. I've known them for years."

Others kept coming up, wanting to know what had happened.

"June Talkington," Mr. Tommy said worriedly, "is the first war casualty from last year's student body. Joined the Medical Corps. Sent to the Mediterranean area after only five months of training. Now they say he's been missing for over a month. We just hope and pray that he isn't dead."

The news swept the campus. All week long people kept asking, "Have you heard anything more about June?"

At Friday assembly, President Hull reported no further word, adding, "All we can do is pray."

Two weeks passed and still no follow-up news on the missing June Talkington.

John DuMond, an Agri bigwig, brought his furloughing brother, Sergeant Lloyd DuMond to assembly. Sergeant DuMond's chest glowed with medals. Proud John rattled them off: "Distinguished Flying Cross, Purple Heart, Air Medal, two Oak Leaf Clusters, and a Presidential Citation.

"My brother will be in the lounge of Wilson Hall at seven o'clock tonight to answer questions," John said.

Josh, like everybody else, was impressed. "I'm goin' to get my cows milked in time to hear him. Bet he'll tell us about being rescued by native girls."

That night the big room was packed with male students, faculty, and cadets. Even Georgie was there. A good spirit prevailed as the questions rained down on the decorated serviceman.

"How many combat missions have you been on?"

Sergeant DuMond scratched his head. "Sixty-five, I think. I'm just one of the crew," he grinned modestly. "A top turret gunner."

"Tell us about one of your most exciting missions."

"Well, I'll never forget the day we started out on our 13th. Our pilot told us he had a feeling something was going to go wrong that day. Somehow our Fortress got away from the rest of the squadron. We had bombed two Jap cruisers, a destroyer, and a transport when Jap Zero fighters came after us like a swarm of bees. We sent three Zeros spinning into the ocean."

"Was anybody hurt?"

"Bullets knocked me to the floor. I got up and nailed another Zero after I was hit in the head and the hand."

Boy, did he keep everybody's attention. "Two of our four engines were shot away, but our pilot kept the plane in the air until he could make a safe landing in the water. We blew up a life raft and pushed it in the ocean. We were in the water 17 hours until an American torpedo boat picked us up."

"Weren't you scared?"

"Sure. Anybody tells you he isn't scared to death when he's surrounded by enemy planes, he's crazy. But I think we do better when we're scared. On one mission our bombardier pulled his lever and dropped his bombs about three seconds after he was shot in the head."

"What's this about being carried out by native girls?"

"That came after another crash landing. Those gals carried our whole crew on litters five days through the jungle to friendly territory. The bugs almost ate us up and lizards kept crawling all over us."

"How many survivors in your group?"

Sergeant DuMond's eyes grew moist and he swallowed hard before answering. "A hundred and five of us were assigned to the Southwest Pacific theater. Only 13 of us are still alive."

"Are you going back?"

"Soon as I get a little rest, if they'll let me. They've offered me a medical discharge, but I'm not ready for that yet."

The questions kept coming for another hour. Finally, the sergeant's brother stood up. "Lloyd's tired and needs to get to sleep. He's staying with me here in the dorm and will be hanging around campus for a few more days. So you'll have other times to talk to him."

Mr. DuLaney had been listening intently to every word. He jumped up. "Let's give the sergeant a big hand. It's fellows like him who are protecting our freedom."

The guys clapped, whistled, and stomped their feet. Somebody broke out with "God Bless America." It was an evening we would not soon forget.

At every weekly assembly President Hull talked about "the brave men who are fighting to keep us free." Sometimes he added, "and the brave women in uniform who are supporting them." Mr. Tommy kept a list of the hundreds of Tech alumni who were serving their country in the military. He urged all students to adopt a serviceman and write him regularly. Mr. Tommy also invited furloughing servicemen to visit the campus as guests of the college. If Mr. Tommy ever mentioned service women, I didn't hear it.

Interscholastic football had been suspended until the war ended. Coach John "Ephod" Tucker, the athletic director, didn't forget the men who had played for him before the war and were now fighting to win the peace. Old Ephod's favorite was Nathan Gordon who had starred at end with the Wonder Boys in 1935. Coach Tucker never tired of relating how Lieutenant Gordon, a Navy man, had won the Congressional Medal of Honor.

"He flew a Catalina with the Black Cat Squadron. A Cat can crawl right out of the ocean and take off on a beach. Just like a big turtle. Ole Nate went in three times and picked up 15 of our men where they were floating in a bay just off the shore of a Japanese-held island. Plucked those Americans right out from under the noses of the Japs."

When Lieutenant Gordon came home on furlough, Coach grabbed him for Assembly. We sang "America The Beautiful" and enjoyed a short football film. Rev. Fritz Goodbar, the pastor of Russellville's First Baptist Church, thanked God for "keeping Brother Gordon safe," then Coach introduced his special guest. "Nathan's the first Tech man to win the Medal of Honor. Let's show him how much we appreciate him." Applause, cheers, and whistles ripped through the Little Theater.

The hero was telling about his job as a pilot of an amphibious Catalina flying boat, when Coach Tucker pulled at his coat tail. "Tell us about the rescue that earned you the Medal of Honor."

"Well," he began modestly, "we heard an army pilot on the radio say that some downed American flyers were floating on a life raft about 40 miles from us. We radioed the pilot to ask him their position.

"We went in three times, each time coming closer to the shore and picked up 15 men all told. I think eight of them were injured. If it hadn't been for the exceptional strength of one of our crew, I doubt if some of them could have been saved." He paused as if to give the impression that his role in the rescue was no big deal.

"Didn't the Japanese shoot at you?" Coach asked.

"Well, yes, they did turn their big batteries loose. Fortunately for us, the ocean swells ran so high that they couldn't take point blank aim. Actually our Cat was in greater danger from the swells than the shore batteries."

At Coach's request, he gave a few more details, but nothing that detracted from the appearance that he and his men were just doing another job.

We all looked pretty meek as we filed out. Howie, for one, allowed that he didn't feel like bragging about his grades. "At least not for a couple of days," he drawled.

As for June Talkington, he made it home safely and picked up his studies from where he had left off.

There was no course offered in patriotism that spring term of 1944, but I discovered that you learn more in college than just the information given out in classrooms.

Chapter 9

"D Day"

Four weeks into my first term at Tech, I walked into Mr. DuLaney's office to ask about the upcoming mid-term test. "Anything and everything we've covered in class and on reading assignments," he said.

Mr. DuLaney shared an office with Raymond "Rabbit" Burnett, the basketball coach and Techionery manager. "Where's Rab — er, Mr. Burnett?" I asked. I didn't tell Mr. DuLaney that I wanted to talk to the coach about trying out for the basketball team in the fall.

To my astonishment, the usually staid Thomas A. DuLaney jumped up and began looking around the room. Under Rabbit's desk. In the closet. Behind a coat rack. "Rabbit? I don't believe Rabbit is here, James." My history professor plopped back in his desk chair, looked over at me and grinned. "Come back and bring a dog. Maybe we can track Rabbit down."

"Yes, sir," I said. "I'll bring ole Shep from Judy."

"And I'll call President Roosevelt in the White

House and ask him to send his dog, Fala, to help us find Rabbit."

I left rubbing my eyes in astonishment that Mr. DuLaney had a sense of humor.

The very next day news swept the campus that Rabbit had resigned to accept a coaching job at Little Rock High School. Tech's postmaster, J.P. Chancey, was to take his place in the Techionery. Athletic Director John Tucker would coach Tech's basketball team.

I knew Coach Tucker only by reputation. Next to President Hull, the big solidly-built man whom some called Ephod was the most admired person on campus. I wasn't a big football fan, but I was told of his exploits as a player by Howie Parish who seemed to know everything about everybody.

"Coach Tucker quarterbacked the Tech football team during the Great Depression," Howie told some of us one day at dinner. "Tech was so outstanding that they even played Army. A special train took people from Arkansas for the game," Howie said. "Coach Tucker broke his collar bone and couldn't play. That's probably the reason we lost the game. Coach transferred to Alabama and led the Crimson Tide to victory in the Rose Bowl."

The weekly assembly in the Little Theater came a couple of days later. At mid-term Dean Turrentine was to present the **E Pluribus Unum** award — a silver dollar — to the top student in each department.

At dinner the day before, Howie was unbearable. "I'm gonna get a silver dollar," he crowed to anybody who came near our table. Josh was so angry that he stood up and moved away with his tray. Marie was so disgusted she could have slapped the braggart. Emma kept trying to get him on a new subject.

The egotistical rascal switched over to me. "'Fesser here's gonna get an award from Miss Massie for the best speaker of Judy English. She's gonna give him 13 pennies, one for each year of his life. Mr. DuLaney's gonna present him with a Bible for showing us where 'Noah looked into the ark and saw.' Mr. Fiser's gonna give 'Fesser a big cigar for tackling ole Georgie."

When Howie paused to take a bite of peas, Marie jammed the spoon back into his mouth. Howie jumped up and spit down the front of her dress. She ran for the washroom, with Howie trailing behind, mumbling, "I'm sorry! I'm sorry!"

The rest of our gang almost fell off our chairs laughing.

Howie did get one of the five silver dollars that was handed out by Dean Turrentine. As he stepped down from the platform, Josh and Marie booed softly. Howie glared at them and slipped back into his designated front row seat.

After the honors' ceremony, Engineer Richard Page from Harrison stepped up before the big microphone and gave an imitation of famed newscaster Edward R. Murrow in reporting the war news from Europe.

Good evening, fellow Americans. I've just been informed that the British government has banned radio and telegraph transmissions from the British Isles. Diplomatic pouches are being opened and censored and foreign diplomats are

forbidden to leave the country. The best
speculation is that the Allies are tightening up
security for the coming invasion of France.

And now, ladies and gentlemen of the
listening audience, I switch you to the Little
Theater on the Arkansas Tech campus in
Russellville, Arkansas where President J.W. Hull
awaits to give us his commentary on the news.

His thinning hair glistening under the lights,
President Hull stepped up to the big mike. "Thank
you, 'Mr. Murrow' for that important information. I
agree with you that the invasion will soon be
forthcoming. We would wish there would be no
casualties, but realistically, we can expect that many
of our finest young men will make the ultimate
sacrifice for victory and world peace. May God bless
our men in service. May God help those of us on the
home front to be faithful in our support."

President Hull glanced down at his notes. His
face furrowed. Something was troubling him.

He cleared his throat twice before speaking again.
"Young men and women, I commend you for your
willingness to give up dorm rooms to the dedicated
service men and women training on our campus.
When the war is over, we hope many of them will
enroll as regular students at Tech. Until then, please
be patient and courteous. For you young dormitory
men that means the lounge in Wilson Hall will
continue to be for the use of cadets only." His eyes
swept around the theater. The lines in his forehead
deepened. "There will be no more scuffling over
territory," he declared.

He cleared his throat again. "One final item

concerns the raising of the flag in front of Wilson Hall. A few mornings ago, somebody sneaked out before daylight and raised a pair of dirty pajamas up the flagpole."

Marie, sitting between me and Josh, giggled. Josh elbowed her in the ribs.

President Hull looked grim. "That was disrespectful to the flag under which so many brave servicemen are fighting and dying. It must not happen again. The flag pole is for the Stars and Stripes."

President Hull then called on Mr. DuLaney to dismiss us with prayer.

I was walking downstairs with Marie to European History when I felt a hand tap my shoulder. Howie Parish. "Hefley, I'm sorry I gave you a hard time at dinner yesterday."

I turned and rolled my eyes at him. "Ya did act like a know-it-all bighead."

"I know. That's what Jeri Lynn said when she turned me down for a movie date last night. She really took the wind out of my sails."

I touched him on the arm. "Thar's plenty of other girls. Ask Emma. She'll go see that movie with ya."

"Yeah, but there's only one Jeri Lynn," he sighed.

Walking side by side, Howie and I strolled into Mr. DuLaney's classroom and took our seats.

Mr. DuLaney called the roll.

Howie addressed Mr. DuLaney. "Sir, when's the invasion gonna take place?"

Mr. DuLaney was off and running. "Y-y-you heard w-what 'Mr. Murrow,' er Richard Page said in

Assembly. He got his information for his newscast from President Hull, who has contacts with some t-op b-b-brass." Mr. DuLaney tapped his desk with his fountain pen. "I predict the invasion will come early in June. Maybe while we're having final exams.

"Today I want to remind you to behave like young adults during the special Agri Day activities."

The Agris always celebrated their big day in early May with a coronation of king and queen, an Assembly program, a tug of war between Agris and Engineers, and a banquet and dance in the evening.

The Assembly program was boring, though Josh didn't think so. When I fell asleep, Josh punched me. "Wake up, 'Fesser, you might jist learn somethin."

An expert in cotton farming was talking about boll weevils. I yawned. Josh punched me again. Five minutes later I was back in dreamland. Josh let me sleep until the end of the program.

The tug of war was more fun. It took place near the Red Barn where the Agris had dug a manure pit. Mr. Tommy was the master of ceremonies and referee.

Volunteers from each club grabbed the rope on opposite sides of the manure pit. "Listen up," Mr. Tommy hollered. "The object is to see who is the strongest. Don't anybody start until I blow my whistle."

I stood on the side with Emma and Marie. Mr. Tommy blew his whistle. "Unh, unh, unh." With Joshua as the front man, the Agris pulled the Engineers toward the pit. Then the Engineers captured the momentum and began dragging the

Agris toward the stinky hole. Suddenly the rope broke, ending the contest.

Time marched closer and closer to final exams. I got nervous just thinking about them, and really wasn't even aware that another day was creeping up on me.

On Friday the second of June - my 14th birthday - I wheeled in from Tech and was surprised to discover that Aunt Jane had a cake in the oven. Then she handed me a letter from Mama which I gobbled up with enjoyment. Aunt Jane noticed my grin. "What'd she say, James Carl?"

"Jist that she's proud of me and that if I was home she'd bake me a cake for my 14th birthday. Mama must really miss me 'cause we never pay much attention to birthdays in our family. The only time I remember her baking me a birthday cake was when I was six and we were living in the log cabin up the creek from Judy. The weather was so hot that we had to sleep on the porch with Daddy's hound dogs."

"What about your daddy?" Aunt Jane persisted. "Did he wish you a happy birthday."

"Daddy ain't one to write. Mama said he was busy gettin' ready for a coon hound field trial on Saturday."

I had to explain a coon hound field trial to Aunt Jane. "Daddy puts up the prize money. Men pay Daddy two or three dollars apiece to enter their dogs. He drags a coon in a sack over a trail and ties the critter up in a tree. The dogs are turned loose on the coon trail a mile back. The first dogs to find the coon win the prizes."

Uncle George stomped in as I was finishing. "Oh, I've heard about them field trials. A feller at work entered his hound dog in one down at Dardanelle and won a hundred dollars."

"Sounds like gambling to me," Aunt Jane remarked as she stooped to pull the cake from the oven.

Uncle George smacked his lips in anticipation. "Dinner won't be ready for half an hour," Aunt Jane noted. "You men folks can go rest on the front porch."

When we came back the cake was iced and sported a pink candle in the center. "I've only got one for you to blow out," Aunt Jane said.

After supper the candle was lit and I blew it out with one puff. Aunt Jane started singing. "Happy birthday to you….Happy birthday to you, James Carl." Uncle George just stood by grinning.

"Thank ya, thank ya," I told Aunt Jane. "Everything would be jist perfect if Mama and Daddy and the kids were here. And ole Shep too," I added. "I shore do miss him."

Saturday I biked to the Tech library and studied all morning for finals in European and Arkansas history. Then I rode back to my boarding house, ate left-over cake, and biked over to the grade school playground to shoot marbles with Lem.

Sunday morning, Aunt Jane fixed a steaming breakfast of bacon, eggs, biscuits and gravy and opened a jar of homemade applebutter. While she was washing dishes, Uncle George lay down for a little nap. I retreated to the living room with a *Superman* comic bought at the Techionery. Along about ten o'clock, I heard Aunt Jane fussing at Uncle

George to hurry up and get ready for church. She peeked her head in the doorway and asked me, "Why don't you come with us, James Carl?"

I slid the comic up under my shirt. "I gotta study for Miss Massie's English test that comes at eight o'clock in the mornin'. That ole biddy's the meanest teacher I ever had in my life."

Aunt Jane stalked up to my bed and wagged her forefinger under my nose. "Don't you go callin' Miss Massie bad names. She's just trying to help you make something out of your life."

I jerked my head back and snorted. "I ain't never gonna take another class under her."

" 'You ain't. You ain't.' Educated people don't say 'ain't,' James Carl."

"They kin say whut they want, but I ain't gonna stop sayin' ain't. Evah'body in my family says ain't, even Mama, 'n she used to be a school teacher."

Aunt Jane snorted her displeasure at me and hollered at her husband. "George, you ready for church?"

Uncle George came shufflin' out, pushing his white shirt into his trousers.

I held up Miss Massie's *Composition and Rhetoric* in front of my face and begin reading loud enough for Aunt Jane to hear as she and Uncle George stepped out the door.

"Who left his books here? Whom left his books here? The nominative form is required because who is the subject of the verb left.

"Whom did Mary call? Who did Mary call? The objective form is used because whom is the object of did call.

"Who…whom…who…whooooom? Szzzzzz."

I must have slept for an hour and a half. The sound of Uncle George's truck snapped me awake. My English book had slid off my knee. I grabbed it up and pretended to be studying. Aunt Jane came in first and saw *Superman* on the floor beside my feet. It must have slipped out of my shirt while I was sleeping.

Aunt Jane picked up the comic and shook it at me. "I didn't know Miss Massie gave a test on *Superman*." She walked on into her bedroom without saying another word.

The next day I got off to another bad start when my bike slipped in a mud hole again. Miss Massie didn't act pleased when she heard me walk in, "squish, squish," leaving a muddy trail behind me. Josh Brown hollered, "Hey, 'Fesser, did you go swimmin' with yer clothes on?"

Miss Massie threw me an icy stare. "Don't you have a change of clothing?"

"Yes'um, but I, ah, didn't have time to go put on clean britches and get back hyar in time to take yer test."

She heaved a sigh and shook her head as if to say, "There's no hope for that boy." Then she began passing out the test papers. "This exam," she smiled, "should be easy for those who have studied the text and paid attention in class."

I defined the eight parts of speech, then got in trouble with subjects and predicates, direct and indirect objects, gerunds and participles. I could only guess at whos and whoms.

To no one's surprise, Howie Parish turned his test in first. "Piece of cake," he told a smiling Miss Massie.

I finished just before the period ended and handed in my paper. Marie came trailing behind me. "How'd ya do, 'Fesser?" she asked when we got outside.

"Right now, I don't wanna know. How'd you do?"

"I'll take another 'C'."

Joshua Brown caught up with us. "I flunked, I jist know I did," he moaned.

"You can always repeat the course," Marie assured us both. "One of the girls in Mr. Turrentine's office told me a Mr. Rollow is coming in the fall to help Miss Massie in the English department." Marie smacked her lips. "Says he's a handsome fellow."

"Cain't think about English no more," I pouted. "We've gotta turn our thoughts to history now."

Just as we were convening for European History finals, news came of the Normandy landing. D-Day at last! Everyone was talking about the war news as we entered the classroom. Who could think about ancient history when history was being made at that very moment in Europe?

Mr. DuLaney tersely gave us the latest news, then had Marie and Jeri Lynn pass out test papers. "Try to concentrate," Mr. DuLaney urged.

The war excitement didn't help my grades. I knew the stuff we'd covered in the history textbooks. It was the questions from the out-of-class required reading that drew blanks in my mind.

Finally the torture was over and I got to leave the class room. I ran to the Techionery where a crowd of students and faculty were gathered around a radio, listening intently to the newscaster.

> Allied paratroopers landed first, then thousands of white, yellow and red parachutes floated down upon captive France. Giant battleships, cruisers, and destroyers stood off the coast, hurling steel projectiles from their big guns. Fifteen minutes after a beaming sun lightened the beaches, the first of 176,000 khaki-clad U.S. and British troops waded ashore.

During invasion week I heard no gripes about cadets and WACs taking over housing facilities. No jokes about running dirty pajamas up the flag pole either.

Thirty-six students made up Tech's 1944 junior college graduating spring class. I didn't stay for the commencement exercises. After my last tests were over at noon on Wednesday, I biked back to the house on L Street and packed up my clothes and books. I'd already checked out with Dean Turrentine. He'd seen my grades and thought it better that I "grow up a little more" before coming back to Tech.

I'd written Daddy to meet me at Lurton. Since Uncle George was at work I struck a deal with Georgie to "taxi" me to the depot for a quarter. Right on the dot he came sweeping up to the house in his convertible. Emma and Marie perched in the front seat beside Georgie. Three Tech girls I knew only by sight waved to me from the back.

My friend Lem was there to wave goodbye. He watched goggle-eyed when ole Carrot Top and five college girls jumped out to help me load up. Emma and Marie tossed my suitcase in the trunk. The other three jammed my bike on top of the bag, leaving the handle bars hanging out the trunk door. Georgie supervised.

I learned later that each "passenger" had paid Georgie a dime apiece just to ride around town in his Chevy convertible.

Aunt Jane got all choked up over my leaving. I kissed her on the cheek and she hugged me tight. "James Carl, you've become like a son to me. When you're ready to come back to Tech, you've got a room here."

The five girls and Georgie were already back in the convertible. "Where do I set?" I asked him.

Marie held out her freckled arms. "Right here," she giggled. I could hear Lem snicker.

She pulled me onto her lap and brushed her lips across my blushing mug. The other girls oohed. Georgie cackled. "Jist like kissin' my little brother," Marie chirped.

We all waved goodbye to Aunt Jane and Lem. Georgie whipped the Chevy convertible around and roared back down L Street . A left on Arkansas Avenue and in less than five minutes they had me at the bus depot.

Uncle George Sutton, the Red Ball driver, was really impressed. "Air all these girls goin' home with you, James Carl?"

I turned pink, just thinking of what Mama and

Daddy might say if they could see me with five girls. I'd never kissed a girl in all my life, unless you'd count my sisters when they were babies.

Marie and Emma carried my bike inside the depot. Uncle George insisted on lifting up my bag himself. He pulled the Red Ball away with Georgie waving and the girls blowing me kisses.

Daddy's Model A wasn't parked outside Sutton's Store when the Red Ball pulled into Lurton, but Daddy came shuffling out the screen door. "You should have been at the bus station in Russellville," Uncle George Sutton told Daddy. "Five girls come to see James Carl off."

"You don't say, George. You don't say," Daddy declared while my face flamed.

"Let's get loaded in, Son," Daddy said. "Yer mama is anxious to see ya. Now bring yer bicycle and foller me."

To my surprise, Daddy carried my suitcase to a glistening Chevy pickup parked by the side of the store. "Bought this truck with money made from selling coon dogs and running field trials," he said proudly.

He pulled the Chevy out into the road. Daddy was almost always in a good mood and today he was feeling especially happy. "Won't be long now 'till the war's over," he predicted. "Ole Eisenhower's got ole Hitler on the run. An' ole MacArthur's breathin' down the back of ole Tojo's neck in the big Pacific ocean."

"Well, I'm lookin' forward to seein' my dawg Shep. How's he doin', Daddy?"

Instead of answering, he pointed to a squirrel running across the road in front of us and braked the truck to a stop. "Daddy," I pleaded, "I ain't been home for over a month. I want to see my dawg and ever'body. You start squirrel huntin' and we won't make Judy 'til after dark."

Without a word he hit the starter and drove on.

Mama, my five sisters, brother Monk, and a boodle of cousins gave me a grand welcome. So did ole Shep who jumped into my arms.

Monk was eying my suitcase and bicycle. "Ya come home to stay?"

"I'm skippin' the summer term. I'll go back in the fall."

That was okay with Mama. "We'll be glad to have you home for awhile," she said.

Mama had a funny look on her face. Like she was holding something back.

"Is something wrong, Mama?" I asked.

What she said set my blood to churning. "Son, we had to sell Ole Shep. A man came by looking for a dog to help round up his cattle. He gave us $20. With you in college, there warn't anybody here to take care of Shep. And we didn't know when you'd be home again."

"The feller ain't comin' fer Shep 'til Saturday," Daddy said. "We thought you might want to tell yer dawg goodbye."

I grabbed Shep by the collar and ran away crying.

Saturday early, I took Shep to the creek and tied him behind a big cedar, thinking that if Mama and Daddy couldn't find him in Judy, they would give the man his money back. However, I didn't reckon with Daddy's record of never, ever going back on a dog deal. Accompanied by the buyer, he tracked us down. With me wailing like a banshee, they took my dog away.

I felt as if my heart were literally breaking. Part of me had been torn away. I could understand better what people were suffering losing their loved ones in battle.

Chapter 10

"Flunked by Miss Massie"

My final report card for the spring quarter came in Monday's South Mail. Mama's face ridged in a tight frown as she read my grades: two Cs, two Ds, and my big fat F in English, a required course.

"Mama, I tried. I jist couldn't pass Miss Massie's final. And I bet I warn't the only one that flunked."

Mama was never one to bad mouth a teacher. But it was a different story when her first born had been flunked, a son who had made As and Bs at Judy High School. "Maybe, I oughta go to Russellville and talk to your Miss Massie about giving you another test," Mama said.

I slowly shook my head. "Mama, you don't know Miss Massie. She's the hardest teacher on campus."

Mama pulled a Tech catalog from a shelf behind the candy counter. She flipped to the course listings and began scanning the pages. "Composition and Rhetoric is required for graduation. Wait!" Mama looked up with a smile. "You can take a required course over."

"Mama, I know that. I jist ain't takin' no more

English under Miss Massie."

"But you've got to have basic English."

"Mama, I ain't takin' Miss Massie. If I have to take her, I ain't goin' back to Tech in the fall."

"Is there another English teacher?"

"A girl I know, Marie, says a Mr. Rollow may start teaching in the fall. I hope I can take him. He couldn't be worse than Miss Massie."

"That'll be good," Mama agreed. "You'll do better after you git some rest this summer. I'll order you some punchboards so you can make a little money. You can't spend all your time on the creek bank this summer."

"Mama, I'd rest a lot better if I had ole Shep back."

"No, son. We took the man's money. Your Daddy will give you one of his dogs to take fishing."

"I don't want one of Daddy's ole hounds."

Mama turned to wait on a customer. I had to accept Shep as being gone. It was the hardest blow I'd had in my young life.

The punchboards came the next Thursday. I put them out on the candy counter immediately and the customers began swarming in. There hadn't been any punchboards in Judy since before I went to Tech. Within a day and a half, the boards looked like sieves.

When I started reeling off all the things I could buy with my profits, Mama interrupted. "Not yet, James Carl. I want you to save money for your college tuition and room rent in the fall."

"Room rent! I can live in the dormitory?"

Mama gave me a little squeeze. "Maybe bein'

with older boys will help you study more."

"Yeah, Mama. I'll do better. I know I'll do better."

I walked up to David Criner's house on the hill above Judy School. My best buddy in high school was at the barn pitching hay to hungry cows. "You home from Tech fer the week-end?" he asked.

"Fer the summer. I'm goin' back to Tech in the fall and stay in the dorm. You oughta come with me. We could be roommates."

David leaned on his pitch fork. "Mother and Dad need me here on the farm. Hey, why don't we go fishin' tomorrow evenin', after I feed the cows and slop the hogs?"

"Suits me."

After supper a small crowd of Judy people gathered around our radio to hear the latest invasion news from Gabriel Heatter:

> There's good news tonight. Allied forces have moved deeper into France. They've got Paris on their minds.

> There's also some sad news, which does not come as unexpected. Lieutenant General Omar Bradley has announced the American casualties of the Normandy invasion: 3,283 dead, 12,600 wounded. Each of those young men is some mother's dear son. Remember the families in your prayers tonight.

I slept late the next morning. When Mama came to wake me up, she wore a grim look. "One of your high school classmates was killed on Normandy Beach."

This could only be Calvin Hill from Cave Creek. I dabbed at my watery eyes. Calvin. The quiet, serious, sandy-haired boy with never a bad word about anybody. No prankster either. Everybody's friend. His sister, Lois, had been in our same class. I wondered how she was taking the death of her brother. Losing a dog suddenly didn't seem so important.

I was wolfing down a peanut butter sandwich when Daddy came in from walking his coon dogs. Mama placed a tender hand on his shoulder and mused, "If the doctors in Little Rock hadn't turned you down, you could have died in that invasion, Fred."

I slipped out and left them to their musings.

David and I went fishing as planned that evening. Dangling crawdads off the Tom Greenhaw Bluff, we snagged six small mouth bass, only three of which were keepers. Mostly we talked about Calvin. "He died fighting for freedom," David said. "If I hadn't had polio, that could have been me."

"Yeah, and if I was four years older, I could have been there."

The fish stopped biting. David grab-hooked an old grandpa frog who wouldn't shut up. I reeled in my bait. "Let's go home," I said. "Ain't nuthin' bitin' down here 'cept gnats."

A new order of punchboards arrived in about a week. Mama again stressed my responsibility: "Keep a record of the profit you make. Don't spend any money without telling me. And when you leave the store, put your boards away."

I arranged the new boards on top of the glass candy counter. Anybody looking for a treat would have to see them.

Uncle Berry Greenhaw shuffled in and surveyed the scene for a couple of minutes. "Believe ah'll try a punch." When he didn't win a prize with three tries, he turned and shuffled off, mumbling, "Waste of good money."

Uncle Berry was the only customer I had that morning. After dinner, Monk and I went fishing. Monk took along his cur dog, Danny Boy, which made me miss ole Shep all the more. Mostly, we killed snakes and caught frogs. The creek was low and clear, the sun bright. The fish weren't biting.

Saturday, when folks came to town with trading and buying on their minds, I made $8.35. I gave Mama $5 for a new rod and reel and stashed the rest in my wallet to apply on the bill for the punchboards.

Sunday afternoon, Daddy took Monk and me and a couple of cousins on an overnight fishing trip to Richland Creek, a sanctuary for bass and moonshiners. I pitched a Heddon River Runt through a hole in the bushes alongside a deep hole. The plug caught on a willow. I pulled to retrieve it and jerked a barbed hook deep into my thumb.

"Yeooww!"

Daddy quickly sized up my situation. "We're a long ways from a doctor. Stick your thumb out to me and hold still."

Before I realized what was happening Daddy had yanked out the hook, taking a plug of flesh from my thumb with it. "Go warsh off the blood in the creek," he said. "You'll jist be sore fer an air er so." No antiseptic. No bandage. I cleaned off the blood and went back to fishing. I forgot the soreness a few minutes later when I caught two 12-inch bass on one cast.

That was my summer. Fishing. Making money with my punchboards. Lounging with the old men on the store porch. Listening to big-league baseball games in the afternoon. Keeping up with the war news at night with Gabriel Heatter, Walter Winchell, and the dean of all commentators, H.B. Kaltenborn. Giving my opinion to anyone who would listen.

One night after newscaster Walter Winchell had signed off, I got out an old splotched geography textbook from Judy school and flipped to a map of France. I pinpointed the recently captured port city of Cherbourg, and ran my forefinger along an imaginary line into the heart of the nation. I would have bet a dollar to a nickel that Allied troopers would enter the French capital by September. If anybody had taken me up on the bet, they'd have lost. On August 24, 1944, Captain Raymond Dronne, made the initial entry. At 10:30 p.m., Captain Dronne's men parked three Sherman tanks in front of the Paris town hall. Declared Gabriel Heatter: "There's great, good news tonight, fellow Americans. Paris is in a state of celebration."

The new school year at Judy began in mid-August. My cousins were busy with books. Speculating about war and politics with the old men got boring. I began counting the days until the fall term started at Tech. I didn't care who I'd have for

English, so long as it wasn't Miss Massie. I just wanted to get back to the big city of Russellville.

Mama was all for me going back. "You've got to finish your education," she kept reminding. "Or you'll never amount to anything."

"Mama, you look tired. Why don't you set a spell?"

"All right," she consented. "I just haven't had much energy lately."

I turned my face away in embarrassment. "Mama, are you in the family way again? You've already got six young'uns, not countin' Daddy and the store to care for."

Mama nodded. "Doc says the little 'un should come about the middle of October."

The front door squeaked. Uncle Ernie Freeman strolled in to get a sack of flour. "When air ya goin' back to Tech?" he asked me. When I told him the next Tuesday, he offered a ride "all the way to Russellville. Except I've gotta detour down to Lonzo's on Richland and pick up some goods fer friends in Russellville."

Uncle Ernie was married to one of Mama's younger sisters. He and Daddy had long been good buddies. They just didn't agree on drinking. Uncle Ernie drank and sold moonshine whiskey. Daddy was under orders from Mama not to ever take a drink. Of course, Uncle Ernie and other imbibers took their swigs in our feed room. Mama didn't interfere, but we knew that she knew.

Mama also knew what Uncle Ernie would be delivering to his "friends" in Russellville. She thanked him for his offer, and said, "Fred and I'd better take James Carl back to school. He's got a pretty big suitcase."

"Aw, pshaw, Hester," Uncle Ernie said, "what er kinfolks fer, 'cept to hep one another. I'm goin' anyway. 'Fesser will keep me company."

Mama was afraid Uncle Ernie would drink and drive and told him so. "Hester," he assured. "I wouldn't risk hurtin' yer boy in a wreck fer a million dollars."

Mama finally, but reluctantly, agreed that I could go with Uncle Ernie.

Tuesday morning turned out cloudy and foggy. Daddy pushed my suitcase into the back seat of Uncle Ernie's old Model T. I shook hands with Daddy, hugged Mama, and kissed my baby-sister, Freddie. My other sisters were at school, where brother Monk was supposed to be.

Mama had already written Dean Turrentine that I was coming back. He'd signed me up for Room 224 in Wilson Hall. My roommate, Mr. Turrentine had replied, would be a first-year student from Fort Smith by the name of Johnny Jack Williams.

Uncle Ernie whirled the crank and the Model T rumbled to life. I climbed in, hollerin', "Bye, ever'body." Uncle Ernie headed up the mountain in the thick fog.

At the south end of Lurton, Ernie turned left down a bumpy road that I'd never been on before. "Goin' to Lonzo's place," he explained.

The Model T's frame shook as he piloted it down a steep, rocky hill, then through a field which lay alongside the headwaters of Richland Creek. He jerked the Tin Lizzie to a stop before an old-timey log house nestled beside a tree-shaded knoll near the water.

A tall, skinny, bearded man came rushing out on the porch hollerin' at his barking hound dogs, "Shet up! Shet up!"

Uncle Ernie piled out of the Model T. "I'll be doin' business here with Lonzo fer a few minutes. Get out if ya want to, James Carl. If anybody ever asks ya, jist remember that ya didn't see nuthin' down here today."

Lonzo pumped Uncle Ernie's hand, while eying me with suspicion. "He's mah nephew, Fred Hefley's boy," Uncle Ernie explained. "I'm givin' him a ride to Tech. He's not 'posed to see a thang."

Lonzo flashed me a gap-toothed smile. "Oh, shore, I know yer Daddy. He's bought coon dawgs off uf me."

Uncle Ernie passed Lonzo a sheaf of bills. Lonzo counted them, then pulled up a rough-hewn plank from the porch, exposing a shallow pit underneath. "Ten gallons, r'at?"

Uncle Ernie nodded.

Reaching into the dirt pit, Lonzo began pulling up gallon jugs. Uncle Ernie carried them to his car, where he tucked them under a blanket in the back seat. Five minutes and the business was done. Lonzo pounded the plank back in place with a hammer, then cast a wary glance at Uncle Ernie. "Jist don't let Fred's boy take any of this lightnin' into the dorm at Tech, er we'll both be in a heap of trouble."

The fog thickened as we drove back to Highway

7, and didn't lift until just before we got to Tech.

I pointed to the flag waving high above Wilson Hall. "The bugler runs it up every morning," I told Uncle Ernie.

He just grunted.

"Jist drop me off right here. I can carry my suitcase into the dorm."

"Ya sure ya don't need any help?"

"Nah."

I sure felt different from the first time I had been left in Russellville. I felt as if I'd come back home.

Chapter 11

"Seven Come Eleven"

I lugged my baggage to the main entrance of the south wing of Wilson Hall. When I opened the door a porky, red-headed kid almost fell against my pinched face. "Uh, excuse me, young fellow," the red-head said. "I was on my way to the Techionery." He extended a puffy hand. "Name's Billy Swanson. An engineering major from North Little Rock. Are you Professor Aulsbury's son?"

Josh Brown's big bulk shadowed the walk behind me. "Naw, Red, believe it or not, he's a student. Ever'body calls him 'Fesser."

"It's good to see ya, Josh. I'm stayin' in the dorm too. Where do I pick up my room keys?" I asked.

Josh pointed into the lounge that had been off limits for civilian students. "See Mr. C.W.C. Aulsbury. He's at a table in there."

I left my bag in the hall and hurried into the rec room to where the bespectacled animal husbandry teacher was sitting at a table. Josh had pointed him out to me once before at the Red Barn: "Mr. C.W.C. Aulsbury," Josh had said, "really knows how to breed cows. He's also a boxer who attended the Naval Academy."

Mr. C.W.C. Aulsbury looked up as I approached. "Well, if it isn't the Mt. Judy kid." He ran a finger down the list of dorm residents. "Here's your key, James Carl. Your roommate is Johnny Jack Williams. Some call him 'Jumping Jack.' A real music bug. Plays for the campus dances. Up the stairs and down the hall. Room 224 is on the left.

"By the way, Mrs. Aulsbury and I live in the resident apartment behind that wall. If you need anything or have any problem at night, just come and knock on our door."

"What about the cadets?" I asked Mr. Aulsbury. "Ain't — aren't they the only ones allowed to use this room?"

Mr. Aulsbury spread his lips in a big grin. "The ban's been lifted. Everybody can use the lounge now.

"Oh, I should warn you that Johnny Jack has a record player and a radio for which he pays an electricity fee. If his playing gets too loud, ask him to turn the volume down. If he won't cooperate, come and see me."

I was only half way up the stairs when I heard the music coming from 224. "Come on an' hear, Come on an' hear Alexander's ragtime band…"

I knocked. No answer. With the music so loud, I figured he must not have heard me. I turned the knob, cracked the door and saw a short, stocky, sandy-haired boy, eyes closed, swinging and swaying, snapping his fingers, singing, "It's the best band in the land. And if you want to hear the…"

I tried getting his attention. "Ahem. Ah. Hey!" He kept dancing. I tapped him on the shoulder.

He opened his eyes and saw my bag. "You must be my roommate, the little kid they call 'Fesser. Right?"

I nodded. He kept on dancing. "I'm Johnny Jack Williams. Or Jumping Jack if you prefer. I can't be still when music's in my head."

Still whirling, he pointed to a bunk. "That's yours." Then to a brown bureau of drawers. "That's yours." And to a little desk. "That's yours."

" '…Come on and hear, come on and hear Alexander's Rag Time Band.' Hey, dig that tune, 'Fesser. Don't you just love it?"

"What is it?" I asked, raising my chirpy voice above the music.

" 'Come on and hear, come on and hear…' Don't you recognize that song? It's from the movie, playing at the Ritz down on Main Street. I've seen that flick eight times. Ethel Merman is in it. Jack Haley, Dixie Dunbar, Chick Chandler. Irving Berlin wrote some of the music. Surely you've heard Irving Berlin's songs.

"Hey, what kind of music do you like, 'Fesser? Jazz? Classical? Big band? Be bop? Opera? Ballads? Rhythm and blues? I like it all."

He paused, waiting for me to answer. "I like Opry," I finally said.

He smiled and resumed dancing. "What's your favorite opera? Carmen? Faust? Madam Butterfly? I just love Porgy and Bess, especially that song, 'I Got Plenty o' Nuttin'.' "

The record ran out. Johnny Jack lifted the tone arm from the revolving turntable and slipped on a new disc. "Here's one of my favorites, 'I Get a Kick Out of You,' from the old Bing Crosby movie, 'Anything Goes.' Hey, wait, you never did tell me your favorite opera."

"The Grand Ole Opry," I piped. "Comin' to you live from Nashville, Tennessee. Uncle Dave Macon and the Dixie Dewdrops. Roy Acuff, Minnie Pearl… I raised my voice to a shrill falsetto. 'Howdy, I'm jist so proud to be hyar.' Oh, I fergot, Minnie don't sing, but she's on the Opry…"

Johnny Jack suddenly began laughing. "You're a killer, 'Fesser. You're so funny. What could be better than the Grand Ole Opry for hillbillies. I love it — for you. But country music isn't my cup of tea."

Johnny Jack slapped on a Frank Sinatra record. "Oh, Danny Boy, the pipes, the pipes are calling/From glen to glen, and down the mountainside…"

"Hey, that's the name of my brother, Monk's hound dog. He got the name from that record."

I began humming the tune. "Dance a little 'Fesser," Johnny Jack urged.

I took a few steps. "I ain't much good at movin' mah feet. Reckon I'd better put mah stuff in mah dresser."

"Suit yourself, 'Fesser. I've gotta go see Mr. Marvin Williamson — he's the band director — about the music for the dance in the Armory. Hey, why don't you get a date and come?"

I screwed up my mug in a frown. "Nah, I ain't

never had a date in my life and don't want one."

"Well, suit yourself," Jumping Jack said and danced out the door.

Josh Brown came by for me just before supper. We strolled across the campus, saying hi to students returning for the new term. As we stepped into the dining hall, I heard two familiar voices coming up from behind. Emma and Marie. Both as crazy as ever. Marie squeezed my thin right arm. "Glad to see you back, 'Fesser. Let's eat together. It's gonna be like old times."

Joe Sidney was at the head of the chow line, saying, "Hello, hello," and, "Good to see you back." Jeri Lynn and Howie Parish waved us over to the table where they were sitting. Marie whispered in my ear, "Hey, look how close they're settin'. Two weeks ago they were both datin' other people."

After supper, the six of us strolled over to the Techionery and watched the jitterbuggers. Marie tried three times to get me out on the floor before giving up. After an hour or so Howie and I walked the girls back to their white-columned residence, Caraway Hall.

The second floor hall was quiet when I got back to Wilson Hall. Obviously Johnny Jack was not in our room. Being a Tuesday night, I clicked on Johnny Jack's radio to hear the goings-on at 79 Wistful Vista. Doc Gamble was arriving for a visit with Fibber McGee and Molly.

DOC: Hello, Molly. Hi ya, Neanderthal.

FIBBER: Hiya, Arrowsmith. Kick yer case of corn cures into a corner and compose your corpulent corpus on a convenient camp chair.

DOC: Thanks, McGee. Your hospitality is
equaled only by your personal beauty...

I opened the door to the hall to get some air. A
distant rattling sound touched my ears. Like someone
throwing gravel against a wall. I ignored the noise
and cocked my ear to hear the McGees.

MOLLY: Had a lot of operations, Doctor?
You look tired.

DOC: My dear, I've had more people in
stitches today than Bob Hope. But tell me, what's
our one-string fiddler doing with the pot-bellied
Stradivarius?

FIBBER: This, my ignorant bone-bender, is
a mandolin...

DOC: If you really get good with that
syncopating cigar box, McGee, and want to run
away and join the gypsies, I'll be glad to pierce
your ears for earrings...

I caught the distant rattle again. Actually it had
never stopped. I closed the door to the hall, but the
noise persisted.

FIBBER: ...When did you become a music
critic, you big fat epidemic chaser?

DOC: Why, you uncultured little faker, I've
got more music in the first phalanx of my left
pinkie than you have in your whole family tree...

As Fibber and Molly faded away, the rattling
sound began assailing my hearing. I got up and
ambled down the hall toward the noise. Coming
closer, I could hear voices. First, Howie Parish:
"Seven come eleven!" Then the red-head I'd met
when coming into the door. "C'mon, c'mon. Bones
do your stuff."

They were obviously shooting dice.

I knocked on the door. The air became deathly still. Then, "Who's there."

"Me. 'Fesser."

Howie cautiously cracked the door, then widened it to let me slip in. Six boys were in the room. One, whom I'd never met, was sipping a bottle of whiskey.

"Wanna shoot some craps?" Howie asked.

Red held up his hand. "How old are you, 'Fesser?"

"Fourteen, but I'm old enough to shoot dice. I run a gambling business in my hometown."

"You from Nevada?"

"Nope, from Mt. Judy up in Newton County."

"I guess it's okay for him to roll the dice," Red conceded. "But no whiskey, or we could get in big trouble giving alcohol to a kid."

I threw down a quarter from my punchboard money. Twenty minutes later, I was a dollar in the hole. I flipped the dice to Red. "You roll 'um. I do better with punchboards."

Heavy footfalls echoed from down the hall, then a knock and C.W.C. Aulsbury's stern voice. "Open up!"

Red grabbed the dice and dropped them in a dirty sock. Howie dropped the whiskey bottle in a dresser drawer, then jumped in a chair and pretended to be reading a book.

I opened the door for ole C.W.C. "I've been hearing a funny noise," he said. "You boys haven't been shooting dice, have you?"

Dead silence reigned.

"Well, I'd better not catch you. The faculty and

administration look upon student gambling with great displeasure. Not to mention drinking."

With concurring nods all around, our resident faculty monitor said good night and closed the door. But a new door had been opened in my life.

I had been back in our room only a minute or so when Jumping Jack returned. "Who're you takin' for the new quarter?"

"I ain't takin' no girl to no dance, that's for sure."

My roommate cackled. "I mean who are you takin' for your teachers?"

I got out my catalog and showed him the courses I had marked: Mr. Tommy, Biology; Miss Clark, Typewriting; Mr. Merrill, Social Science; Mr. DuLaney, Western History; Mr. Rollow, English, and Mr. Fiser for Phys. Ed. for men.

Jack had professors Tommy, Merrill, Fiser and Rollow with me. The rest of his teachers were in the music department.

We talked about the respective merits of the professors we had in common. "I've asked around," Jack told me. "Everybody who's had Mr. Tommy says he wouldn't flunk a flea. Coach Fiser smokes stinky ole cigars. Mr. P.K. Merrill is the weightiest guy on campus. I wouldn't want to tangle with him in a fist fight. Rollow's a new guy. Nobody seems to know much about him, except the girls who've seen him think he's a 'darling'."

"Rollow has to be easier than Miss Massie. That ole biddie clipped my wings in the spring. I ain't never takin' any subject under her again."

Jack shot me a stern big brother look. "'Fesser,

mah boy, you'd better change your attitude if you're ever gonna make it through college. And learn to speak decent English. 'Ain't never takin'' won't cut the mustard."

Jack saw he'd made me uncomfortable and quickly changed the subject. "I can hardly wait 'til football starts up. Mr. Williamson, the band director, thinks Coach Tucker will be holding scrimmages this fall. Then if the war is over by next summer, Tech will be ready for conference play."

Jack and I talked until 11 o'clock then he played a Frank Sinatra record. "You know who Sinatra is, don't you?" my roomie asked.

"Sure. The girls are crazy about him. Marie Singleton told me she'd seen every one of his movies. I think he sounds like a sick calf."

Jack grimaced. "He does drive girls wild. Couple of years ago in New York City, there was a riot at his first performance. Ten thousand bobby-soxers screaming for autographs. Some tried to tear off his clothes."

"He still sounds like a sick calf. I'd rather hear Roy Acuff."

The next day was registration. I got the classes I wanted, with Mr. Rollow scheduled at eight o'clock in the same room where Miss Massie had persecuted me during the spring term. When I arrived for the first day of class, Marie was there and waved me over to sit next to her. I looked at her knowingly. "You flunked Miss Massie, too?"

"Yep and look who I got now. Sir Walter Raleigh. Look at him standing up there talkin' to that new gal.

Isn't he handsome?"

Ignoring her adulation, I pointed to his name on my class card. "John, not Walter. Rollow, not Raleigh."

"Yeah, but he is such a Prince Charming. And he isn't wearin' a wedding ring."

The bell rang. Professor Rollow stood in front of his desk and flashed an assuring grin. "I understand that some of you have been down this road before with Miss Massie."

Marie froze, fearing he was going to call names. All he said was, "I'm not going to hold that against you. I don't want to know who is taking freshman English over."

When he said that, Marie practically gave herself away with a sigh of relief.

He called the roll, carefully enunciating each name and making comments about some of the places we were from. When he came to me, he pronounced my hometown, Judy. "Did you know Doctor Walter Sexton?" he asked. When I nodded, he added, "Well, he's our doctor in Dover now."

He took half the first period getting to know us. Then he brought tears to my eyes in telling about his country mother. "She was eight and the oldest of five children when her mother died. She virtually became the head of the household.

"Mother was 20 when she married my daddy. I was only two-and-a-half when he died from typhoid fever. I was an only child. Mother supported us by teaching school.

"I took the first eight grades in a one-room school,

then I started high school in Dover and made a D in English. Thank God, for the English teacher who joined Mother in inspiring me to go on and get a good education."

John Rollow's mother reminded me of how my mama had always worked so hard and she had sacrificed for her children, too.

"I hope I can teach you some English," Professor Rollow continued. "I hope I can convince you of the necessity of a college education, unless you're just planning on going back to your little country town and live there the rest of your life. There you can say 'I seen,' 'ain't gonna do nuthin',' and 'had did hit' all you want. You can talk like that and they'll take you as you are.

"Or you can get a good education and make your family proud. For that you'll need to start with the basics. And there's nothing more basic than English.

"Learning English is a lot like learning to drive an automobile," he said. "You take it a step at a time until you don't even have to think, 'Now, I've got to put my foot on the clutch.' "

I glanced at Marie. She was enraptured.

"Now, where shall we begin?" Mr. Rollow asked rhetorically. "Can you tell us, Mr. Swanson?"

Red flashed a smug smile. "With the eight parts of speech, sir."

"Correct. At our next class meeting I will give you an exam on those eight parts, their identification and their function. If you don't know this already, consult your textbook." He glanced at his watch. "I'm going to let you out five minutes early. If anyone has a question, see me up here."

Silly Marie made a beeline for his desk. Out of curiosity I trailed along behind her. "Mr. Raleigh, uh Mr. Rollow," she chirped. "Will your test be multiple choice? I'm better at picking out the right answers."

"Some of the questions will be multiple choice. Others will take a different form."

He turned to another inquirer. Marie hung by like a vine reaching out for a tree limb. I finally got tired of waiting on her and walked into the hall where Red and Jumping Jack Williams were discussing the new English teacher. Whitey, the Baptist Student Union recruiter, walked up with a stack of papers.

"Hey, you guys, the BSU is gonna have a wiener roast at our minister's house tomorrow evening. A get-to-know-one-another thing. Red, would you and Jack slide one of these invitations under each door in Wilson Hall? I have a couple of girls putting them out at Caraway."

"I'll take the south halls," Jack said immediately, "and Red can do the north wing."

"And you'll both be at the wiener roast, Monday night?" Whitey pressed.

"Wouldn't miss it," Red declared. "I promised my mother and minister that I'd get active in the BSU."

I didn't say a word. Crap-shooting, whiskey-drinking Red and dancing Jumping Jack were both Baptists!

Whitey touched my skinny elbow. "You're invited too, 'Fesser. You don't have to dress up. Come as you are."

"He can come with me," Jack offered.

I began edging backward. "Naw. I've got something else to do, I may go see 'Young Abe Lincoln' down at the Ritz."

"You can see Lincoln another night," Red said.

Josh came to my rescue. "You got Mr. Tommy for biology at ten o'clock?"

I nodded.

"Let's go have a coke at the Techionery. We can walk across to Bailey Hall from there."

I took off with Josh. We sipped our cokes as we sat in a booth and talked. Above the noise of the juke box and the jitterbuggers, he told me how much he appreciated Mr. Tommy. "I know a dozen boys who would have dropped out of school if he hadn't helped them," Josh said.

Four girls came trooping in, Marie, Emma, and two Marie introduced as Pansy and Charlotte.

Marie and Emma immediately began teasing me about dancing. When I told them, "I ain't no good at dancin'," Josh shot back, "He ain't no good with English, either." That set Marie to talking about "that divine Sir Walter Rollow."

Pansy, a petite little stalk of about my height, kept eying me. Finally, she said, "'Fesser, I bet you can too dance." Whereupon she grabbed my bony arm, jerked me out on the floor, and started jittering to the music of "Chattanooga Shoe Shine Boy." I took a couple of off-balance steps, got my right foot tangled behind my left ankle, and fell over into Emma's lap.

At least Josh felt sorry for me. He chose that time to reach down a big hand and say, "Come on, 'Fesser, let's go see Mr. Tommy." I skittered out behind Josh with the girls trailing after us. They were headed for biology in Bailey Hall too.

For some unknown reason Josh started running. "Hurry up, 'Fesser, I wanna show you somethin'."

I followed him up the stairs to the second floor and into Mr. Tommy's classroom. "Look to yer left," he said.

I did and saw a real human skeleton hanging from a hook on the wall behind the door. I'd never seen one before.

Josh ran and got behind the skeleton. "Go out and come in the door again," he instructed.

I did as Josh said. As I entered, I felt bones grab my neck. Whirling around, I saw that Josh was maneuvering the skeleton like a puppet. "Now get back here and do it to that girl Pansy who made a fool of you in the Techionery," he challenged. He moved out into the room. "I'll stand over here and whistle when she steps in and you grab her with the skeleton."

I took Josh's place behind the door. Through the crack, I could hear students coming up the stairs.

A couple of boys came in, then Marie. Josh whistled. Pansy was right behind her. I reached out the skeleton arms. "Gotcha," I shouted. Pansy screamed and jumped out of my bony clutch.

I squealed in triumph.

Pansy swung her biology book at me. I ducked. Marie grabbed her arm to keep her from striking at me again. "Cool down, gal. 'Fesser's just a kid. He didn't mean you any harm."

About that time Mr. Tommy sauntered in, a thatch

of white hair angling across his forehead. He rolled himself a cigarette from a Bull Durham sack, brushed the tobacco specks off his shirt, and lit his smoke.

Peering through the smoke at us, he took a couple of long drags, glasses poking over his nose.

He picked up his student roll card. "Now some of you I know and some of you I've never laid eyes on before. I'm gonna go down the roll and read out the names. When I come to you, I want you to tell me where you're from and a little somethin' about your home. Most times I'll have been to where you're from. We'll see."

He glanced at the roll card. "Pansy Atchison. The girl that the skeleton grabbed."

Pansy blushed. I pretended to be looking out the window.

"Tell us where you're from, Miss Atchison."

"I'm from Morrilton."

"I've been through there a thousand times on my way to Little Rock," Mr. Tommy said. "What is Morrilton famous for?"

"Sam Houston lived there once with his Cherokee Indian wife," Pansy declared. "My great-great grandmother was a Cherokee and a cousin to Sam Houston's Indian woman. You want to hear more?"

Mr. Tommy held up his hand. "Save ole Sam for Mr. DuLaney in Arkansas History," he said.

Nine names later, Mr. Tommy came to me. "'Fesser, alias James Carl Hefley, tell us where you're from."

"Mt. Judea."

Mr. Tommy dropped his cigarette butt in an ash

tray and began rolling another. "You're trying to act smart, 'Fesser. Pronounce the name the way everybody says it."

"Judy."

"Why was it named Judy?"

"For Judy Mountain which was named after the, uh, Judea of the Bible."

"I've been to Mt. Judy," Mr. Tommy said. "They play horseshoes there on Saturdays and checkers every day of the week."

Mr. Tommy moved on through the alphabet. He finished at ten minutes before the bell with a perfect score. He'd visited and knew something about every one of our home towns.

He pitched the stub of his last roll-your-own into the ash tray on his desk, strolled over to the blackboard and wrote ROCK and BIRD. "What's the difference?" he asked.

Pansy's hand shot up. "One is a living thing and the other is dead."

"Very good. You learned in high school that biology is the study of living things. What can birds do that rocks cannot? Besides fly."

Pansy answered that too. "Birds can make life." She was a female Howie Parish. "Rocks can't."

"So what is biology?" Mr. Tommy asked, adding, "Let's have somebody else answer besides Miss Atchison."

"Biology is the study of living things," Marie declared triumphantly.

Mr. Tommy glanced at his watch. "Quick, now, what are the two divisions of biology?"

"Botany and zoology." I remembered that from science class at Judy High School.

"Very good. You are all smart cookies. Now for Friday, I want each of you to bring me a specimen of a living thing. It can be a plant, a bug, but no pigs or hound dogs, ya hear. You can bring it in a little tobacco sack like the one I've got here, in a Prince Albert can, mount it on a card, or whatever."

The bell interrupted. Mr. Tommy waved his arms. "Now, all of you get out of here and don't come back without your specimens."

Josh walked out between me and Marie, saying, "Didn't I tell ya that Mr. Tommy would be fun? Didn't I tell ya?"

At the 11 o'clock assembly, Josh, Marie and I sat on the same row with Georgie Maloney and three other girls. Georgie leaned over toward Marie. "Wanna go for a spin around town tonight in my convertible?"

Marie grinned back. "You bet." She looked at the three new girls. "Are they goin' too?"

"Yep," Georgie said. "The more, the merrier." Georgie winked at me. "You can come too, 'Fesser. I won't even charge you 'cause you don't take up much room."

The crowd stilled as President Hull welcomed both old and new students to the beginning of the new term. Mr. Hull then led us in a salute to Old Glory and a prayer for the "protection of our boys fighting for freedom on the world's battlefronts."

Mr. DuLaney gave the war report. "The invasion of France has turned into a landslide," he declared.

"Our troops are pounding the outer perimeter of the Siegfreid Line. They'll soon be in Germany!"

President Hull introduced a new faculty member who towered over everyone else on the platform. I had seen him during the spring term sitting with the cadets at lunch.

"Mr. Pierce K. Merrill will be teaching social science," President Hull said. "He's no stranger to this campus. He served as our aeronautics administrator for the Naval Cadet program for the past two years. Before that he was a high school coach, teacher, and superintendent. And I might mention that he was born at Harrison and, like me, is a Methodist," he smiled.

President Hull looked down at Coach Tucker, seated on the front row. "Coach Tucker has some good news for us."

Ole Ephod didn't need a microphone. His strong voice easily carried to the back row. "You all know," he said, "that we haven't had a football season since 1941. I've met with our board of trustees and they agreed with me that this war is not going to last forever. When victory comes, we're gonna be ready for state conference play. The board voted their approval for us to begin practice, starting next Monday afternoon at four p.m. I've already contacted some of the best prospects, but walk-on's will be welcome."

Coach Tucker lifted his fists. "Go, Wonder Boys! Go, Wonder Boys!"

President Hull jumped to his feet. "Go, Wonder Boys!" Faculty and students joined Mr. Hull and

Coach Tucker. "Go, Wonder Boys! Rah! Rah! Rah! Go, Wonder Boys!" thundered through the crowd.

Georgie shouted loud enough to be heard two rows up, "I'll be there, coach! I'm goin' out for football!"

I whispered to Josh in disbelief. "Georgie play football? I put him on the ground every time in phys. ed. last spring. I can do it again."

Josh poked me in the ribs. "You gonna try out?"

"Nah," I said. "I ain't heavy enuff for football. I've got my sights set on basketball."

Josh laughed out loud. "'Fesser, if you make the basketball team, I'll eat a dozen grasshoppers."

We headed down the stairs with the rest of the crowd. As we stepped outside on our way to the dining hall, I grabbed a tiny green grasshopper from the lawn and handed it to Josh. "You can start with this 'un."

Josh shoved my hand back against my lips. "Eat it yer'self, 'Fesser."

I jerked free and ran toward the dining hall. "Last one in's a rotten egg."

Josh didn't even bother to chase me.

Typewriting 113B came after the noon meal. Miss Dorothy Clark was again the teacher. She gave us a speed test. I scored 62 words a minute. Marie and Emma didn't break the 50 mark. Boy, did I ever gloat as I pranced around them as we walked down the hall to Mr. Merrill's Survey of Social Science.

The class room was fast filling up. I parked my skinny frame between Howie and Marie. Howie's real heart throb, Jeri Lynn, occupied a chair two rows in front of us. Next to her was her current beau, husky Jim Bradley. Howie couldn't stand him. She pressed her shoulder against Jim, causing Howie to emit a soft moan. Howie could be melodramatic.

The room filled completely, with three chairs brought in from another room. Mr. Merrill was flying high.

Marie eyed the teacher's muscular frame and granite face rimmed by thick, wavy black hair. "He could pass for a movie star," she sighed.

He called the roll. Each student answered "yes" or "here" in a respectful manner until he came to "Mr. George Maloney." Georgie yelped like a dog.

"Repeat that, please," Mr. Merrill requested.

"Yep, uh, I mean, yes, sir."

Mr. Merrill's eyes twinkled. "That's what I hoped you'd say, young man."

No one else answered with an impudent "yep."

"This class," Mr. Merrill began, "is about people. What can be more fun than studying how people relate to one another? That's what sociology is all about. Relationships. How people associate with each other and in groups. How groups relate to other groups. Groups such as families, churches, labor unions, colleges, athletic teams. And on a larger scale, nations, races, people who speak a common language. I think you get the idea."

Jeri Lynn was snuggling even closer to her latest conquest. Howie was gnashing his teeth.

Mr. Merrill's eyes had been on Jeri Lynn and Jim all along. Our professor cleared his throat twice to get their attention. "Ahem! Ahem! It appears that two of our class members are relating to each other very well. In the proper place that's quite all right. But in class, your manner of relating is, uh, distracting to your instructor and fellow students."

Jeri Lynn blushed a rainbow of colors and sat up straight. Jim did likewise. Mr. Merrill began shuffling his notes as if nothing had happened. Marie and a couple of other girls giggled. Howie stared straight ahead with a pained, dead-pan expression.

Mr. Merrill then gave us a briefing on reading assignments, tests, and grading for the semester.

That evening I talked Jumping Jack into going with me to see "Young Abe Lincoln" at the Ritz. I liked the part where Abe declined a dance with Mary Todd at a party by saying, "The only dancing I've ever done is behind a plow."

"That's me," I told my roomie.

Jack liked Abe, but said the doleful background music ruined the movie for him. "It was awful," he said. "Sounded like a funeral."

Back in our room Jack slapped on a big band record and went prancing across the floor. When Benny Goodman began hitting the high notes of "Goody Goody" with his clarinet, I slipped down the hall to Red Swanson's where six guys were engaged in a lively crap game. At two a.m. and 75 cents poorer, I slipped back to Room 224. The record player was still spinning. Jack lay sprawled across his bed with his clothes on, snoring away.

Thursday, I had only one class, Western History, at nine o'clock in the morning. Mr. DuLaney called the roll and passed out the semester schedule. Then he picked up his notebook and began by giving us a rough outline of the historical events and developments in Western history which we would cover. "All th-th-these events should be very interesting to you because this terrible war, young folks, is a b-b-big part of Western history. War is about people who die for their country believing their cause to be right."

He sketched the roots of Western thought in Judaism, Greek history, Christianity, and the Roman Empire. He was traipsing through the Dark Ages when I slipped into dreamland. A tap on the head from Mr. DuLaney's pointer brought me back to reality. I stayed awake through the Reformation, then I slept until the bell jarred me awake.

Mr. DuLaney stopped me as I was stumbling out of the room. "Boy, didn't you g-g-get any sleep last night?"

"Yes, sir, I mean, not much, sir. I went to see 'Young Abe Lincoln' at the Ritz. Then my roommate played records until two o'clock." I didn't tell Mr. DuLaney that I was in Red Swanson's room shooting dice while Jumping Jack was spinning discs.

Mr. DuLaney eyed me gravely. "You should speak to Mr. Aulsbury about your roommate's lack of consideration."

"Yes, sir, I will, sir."

"This time I'll excuse you, but if you fall asleep again in my class, I'll have to put a mark in my grade book."

It was clear that my new "hobby" wasn't making me a better student.

Chapter 12

"Gambling Fever"

On the way out of class one morning, Josh Brown caught up with me. "You goin' on the college bus to the outing on Petit Jean Mountain tomorrow?"

"Yeah. I wouldn't miss it, since it don't cost nuthin'. 'Sides, Mr. Tommy says there's a lake up there, and I can take my rod and reel."

"Whatcha gonna do tonight?"

"Doodle around, I don't have a quarter to get into a movie. Mama's dollar hasn't come this week."

"I'm broke, too," Josh admitted.

Physical Education for Men 121B, came later that afternoon. Coach Paul Fiser, sporting his trademark stinky cigar, ran us through a routine of pushups and situps, then we divided into teams for a little football.

As I had in the spring, I lined up against Georgie. When Coach Fiser blew his whistle, I rammed a skinny shoulder against Georgie's chest. To my surprise, he bounced me back on the grass like a rubber ball.

Georgie stood over me grinning. "Fooled you, didn't I? You figured I was still an ole softy."

"What happened?" I gasped.

"While you were back in Judy goofin' off during the summer, I was workin' out, doing weight lifting and running wind sprints. I'm gonna go out for football next Monday. When Tech starts playing in the conference again, I'm gonna be on the varsity team."

Georgie, a varsity football player? I couldn't believe it.

"Hit me again," he hollered.

I did and he bounced me on the grass a second time.

Georgie reached down and pulled me up. "Wanna go ridin' around after supper, then see 'Casablanca?' It's playin' at the Ritz."

"Is it a funny movie?"

"It isn't about hillbillies, but it's patriotic. I saw it in Little Rock when it first came out. Humphrey Bogart and Ingrid Bergman are the stars."

I turned up my pockets. "No mon, no fun. Mama didn't send me any money this week."

Georgie threw me his possum grin. "I'll loan you a quarter and buy you some popcorn. We'll load up in front of the dorm and go ridin' before the movie."

At supper I got sidetracked by talking about fishing with Josh. Suddenly I remembered Georgie's invitation. "Ooops, we'd better scoot, if we're goin' with Georgie to see Bogart and Bergman in 'Casablanca'."

"Who's we?" Josh sputtered. "Georgie didn't invite me."

"Oh, come on," I urged. "He'll have room."

Josh still declined. I hurried out of the dining hall

and trotted across the campus to where Georgie always parked. He saw me coming and honked. "Hurry up, 'Fesser."

I ran and jumped in back with Emma and Marie. Pansy and an older guy I hadn't met were in front.

The guy turned and stuck out a big paw over the seat. "I'm Troy Morrison. Got a medical discharge from the Army and enrolled late on the G.I. Bill. Red Swanson says you're a pretty good crap shooter."

"Nah, I'd rather play cards."

"Poker or Blackjack?"

Actually, I'd never played either game. At least not for money. I couldn't let him know that, so I said, "Blackjack."

"I'm a Blackjack man myself," Troy said. "I'm in 124, right underneath the nosiest room in the dorm. Come by sometime and we'll play a few rounds."

"Yeah, sometime." I didn't tell him that the noisy room was mine.

Georgie hit the gas pedal. The sudden momentum threw me against Emma. She squealed and pushed me against Marie. Marie shoved me back. "Hey, hey, stop it," I hollered.

Georgie swept across the bridge over Engineer's Creek, zoomed on to Main, and whipped west, away from downtown. "We spotted Whitey Sampson, going into the First Baptist Church with a bunch of other well-dressed people. Georgie honked twice. "Hey, Whitey," I hollered. " 'Casablanca' is playin' at the Ritz. Come and go with us."

Whitey turned and waved back to us. Marie and Emma threw him kisses as he and his church friends hurried on inside.

Georgie drove on to the western edge of town, honking at people, with me and the girls in the back seat hollering. Pansy and Troy sat in the front seat all prim and proper.

Five miles down the road, Georgie braked and whipped the Chevy around, kicking up gravel as he headed back to town.

"Wheeeeeeee. Wheeeeee." A Russellville cop pulled us over and checked Georgie's license. "You people from Tech?" he asked. "Yes, sir," Georgie piped respectfully.

The cop pointed at me. "That kid, too?"

"'Fesser's from Tech too. He's just little for his age," Marie fibbed. "He's really 22."

The cop cast a sharp eye back at Georgie. "Don't let there be a next time, or I'll have to give you a ticket for reckless driving. And notify the dean's office, too."

Georgie drove meekly back down Main and parked a block from the Ritz. The cop car rolled slowly by, as we jumped out and headed for the show. Georgie paid for me, Emma, and Marie. Troy shelled out for Pansy. We followed the crowd inside, Georgie, Emma, Marie and I were giggling, with Pansy and Troy still acting like grown-ups.

The curtain lifted and the screen came alive with a cartoon. Georgie and Troy bought popcorn for all of us. We saw an adventure serial, the newsreel and "previews of coming attractions" Then came the main feature with Ingrid Bergman as the love interest and Humphrey Bogart playing the role of the cynical drifter working as a barkeep in the exotic Moroccan city.

Troy and Pansy excepted, the rest of us whispered through much of the show. Troy chuckled only when the police officer came to question Rick in the saloon.

"What are you doin' here, Mister?"

"I came to Casablanca for the waters."

"Waters? What waters? We're in the desert."

"I was misinformed."

Emma and Marie emitted a long sigh when Bogy began falling for Bergman. "That man," Marie whispered, "can romance me any time."

Then they both cried when the girl took off in the plane and Bogy gave his memorable last line to the policeman: "This could be the beginning of a beautiful friendship."

The show was over by nine. We shuffled out into the lobby. Emma, Marie, Georgie, and Troy couldn't wait to light up. Pansy and I rushed out the door gasping for air. When Pansy said, "Smokin' is stupid," I looked at the slight stick of a girl with new respect.

Marie came out pushing Georgie ahead of her.

"Why'd you get so love sick over that bartender?" I asked.

Marie glared at me. "'Fesser, you wouldn't know love if you saw it walking down the street."

"Hey, let's go get a shake," Georgie suggested.

I began pretending I was sick. "I don't feel well, Georgie. Take me back to the dorm."

Actually I didn't want the girls to know that I was flat broke. Troy seemed to catch on, for he said, "Come on ever'body. Let me treat. I've got some bucks left from my mustering out pay." A strawberry milk shake quickly cured my sickness.

We got back in plenty of time before the girls' Friday night curfew. Georgie pulled a football out of the trunk and wanted to play catch under the street lights. "I need all the practice I can get," he said.

Troy said no thanks and left to walk Pansy back to Caraway Hall. I tossed Georgie a couple of balls while Emma and Marie stood around star gazing. The girls soon got tired of this. "We're goin' to the dorm," Marie said sharply. And with that she and Emma turned on their heels and started walking.

On impulse, I ran and caught up with them. Georgie just called out goodnight and headed for the men's dorm.

Marie, Emma and I sat on the steps of Caraway with other students who didn't want to go in until the last minute. About 10 minutes to 11, we heard familiar voices. "Well, how about that," Emma whispered. "Looks like Jeri Lynn and Howie are lovebugs again. For Howie, I guess miracles never cease."

"Humph!" I snorted. "I don't think they're lovebugs. I think they're just humbugs."

I still wasn't sleepy and felt lonesome since Jumping Jack had gone home for the weekend to play records for his high school's homecoming dance. I knocked on Red's door and got no answer. I walked downstairs and tried 124. Troy, the ex-Marine hadn't come in yet. I drifted down to the lounge and peeked in on two students playing ping pong.

Since neither invited me to play, I went to my room and hit the hay. I fell asleep thinking of the next day's outing on Petit Jean Mountain.

I forgot to set my alarm, and woke up late. The

clock said three minutes after eight, meaning I had twelve minutes to get on the Petit Jean bus. I jerked on a pair of overalls and a denim shirt, jammed my feet into ball shoes, grabbed my reel and rod and a match box of hooks and sinkers, and took off running.

Felix, the driver, had the motor running and was pulling away, when I pounded on the door. Mr. Tommy saw me from his front seat perch and told Felix to stop and let me in. Miss Lela Jane Bryan, chairman of the sponsoring Tech Social Committee, sat behind her beau, Mr. Tommy. In back of her was Joe Sidney, the cook from the dining hall. He and two of his assistants had the food for the outing.

I put my fishing gear down at the front and elbowed my way to a seat in the last row. Peering through the dusty back window, I saw a trail of faculty and student cars, with Georgie and a convertible full of girls, including Emma and Marie, bringing up the rear.

I smashed my nose against the glass & made a face as Felix drove east along Highway 64 to Morrilton, then turned south to cross the brown Arkansas River. From there he led the line of cars up steep Petit Jean Mountain, stopping at a rocky outcropping that overlooked the river valley stretching far below.

Mr. Tommy jumped out, his trademark roll-your-own cigarette dangling from his mouth. "Hold it! Hold it! Let's all assemble beside the bus. Don't anyone go running off."

When the rest had piled out of their cars, Mr. Tommy pulled the smoke from his mouth. "Now, we don't want anyone falling off the mountain. Keep back from the edge. If you must look down, crawl out and stick your head over. Everyone understand?"

"Yeah, Mr. Tommy," we chorused.

He pointed to Josh and Howie. "You big boys be the police. If you see someone getting too close to the edge, holler at them. If they don't back up, holler at me, and I'll pull 'em back."

I found a trail leading around and back under the big rock outcropping that gave me an idea. I eased down, circled back under the rock, and began yelling, "Help! Help." The people on top thought somebody had fallen. I heard Mr. Tommy calling for a rope, then Miss Bryan began checking the roll of students who had signed up for the outing. Grinning, I scurried back up the trail fast and answered when she came to my name. Fortunately, nobody had seen me duck down the trail.

By now it was going on ten o'clock. Miss Bryan allowed that we should "be on our way to the park where we'll eat lunch. From there we'll go to the lake for swimming and whatever." She glanced at me, then at my rod and reel. "And maybe 'Fesser can catch a fish or two."

Marie pushed past me to get on the bus. "C'mon, 'Fesser," she said, "we can sit together."

I looked at her with raised eyebrows. "Ain't you ridin' with Georgie?"

"Not on this mountain. That boy's crazy."

We ate in a leafy park four or five miles further back on the mountain. Then we explored a cave house a short hike from the park. Naturally, I had to tell everybody within hearing distance that there were much bigger and deeper caves in Big Creek Valley. "I got lost in one once," I said, hoping that somebody would ask for a recital of the event. Nobody did.

The boy-girl ratio at Tech hadn't improved, since the war was not over. Marie struck out with a couple of boys, then dropped back to walk beside me. She cast a curious eye at Mr. Tommy and Miss Bryan who were strolling along ahead of us. "One of the faculty members told me they've been courting for over five years. I wonder if he's ever held her hand."

On impulse, I grabbed Marie's hand. "Now you can't say I haven't held yer's."

"Oh, 'Fesser, you remind me of my little brother. He likes to wear overalls and fish and catch bugs just like you. The only difference is you don't call me names, not even when I leave you to talk to another boy."

"That's cause I feel sorry for you. You don't always have boys hanging over you, like Jeri Lynn. Look at her and ole Howie over there; he's mooning over her like a love-sick calf."

"Yeah, and next week she'll be breakin' his heart," Marie said. "Me — I'm a one woman man, if I could find the right man."

Mr. Tommy got everybody back by the bus where Miss Bryan briefed us on the lake visit. "Those who brought suits can go swimming. Just don't swim out into water over your head. The rest of us can find a chair and sit on the dock."

I held up my rod and reel. "Anybody wanna go fishin'?"

Marie and Emma and a girl named Louise tagged along. None of the boys were interested in fishing. "They just wanna see the beauty parade," Emma said. She pointed to Georgie who had just come out of the male dressing room sporting a carrot-colored swim suit that matched his hair. "That one especially."

With the three girls following, I led the way along the lake's edge to where the water deepened around some mossy rocks. I cast out a Heddon River Runt plug and let Emma reel it in. Then I let the other girls have a try. Marie caught a weed.

I'd had the foresight to bring along an empty pop bottle. "Maybe the fish will like grasshoppers," I proposed. "Let's catch some in the grass back there."

The three girls followed me into a grassy field that ran up close to the lake shore. A big yellow-bellied, long-horned hopper popped up in front of me, landing about six feet out. I pounced on the hopper with both hands and stuffed it in the bottle which I'd ask Marie to hold.

The hoppers were everywhere. I grabbed up another. Marie and Emma caught two each. Then Louise caught the biggest of the lot.

We hurried back to the rocks. "I'll show you how to do it, then you can each try your luck," I told the girls.

I tied on a hook, strung on a hopper, attached a red and white bobber to the line, shucked off my shoes, rolled up my britches legs, and waded out and climbed up onto a rock that extended into the blue lake water.

"Watch the bobber," I instructed the girls.

I'd no sooner closed my mouth when the little plastic ball disappeared under the water. "'Fesser, you've got a bite," Louise yelled, as if I didn't know.

I set the hook. My rod bent half double. Round and round the rock the fish rolled, trying to break loose, while the girls shouted encouragement to me.

I pulled out the fish and held it up. "It's only an eight-inch-bass. Too small to keep." I dropped the little bugger back in the water.

"Let me try my luck," Louise requested.

I strung on the big grasshopper she had caught and handed her the rod. She kicked off her shoes and waded out to the rock. I put the rod in her hand, holding my fingers tight on the line in the reel spool. Releasing her arm, I said, "Now you try it. Place your fingers on the line in the spool, whip the rod out, turn loose of the line, and let it go."

She performed like a professional, but caught only one undersized bass. Then she lost her balance and fell into water up to her waist. I slid off the rock after her and helped her back to shore. "You didn't need to do that," she said. "But thanks anyway."

I squeezed water from the legs of my britches. Emma and Marie took Louise into a patch of bushes and wrung out her skirt. She reappeared with a big smile. "Let me have another try, 'Fesser." I was about to tell her that we'd probably scared all the fish away when Felix, the bus driver, began honking his horn. It was time to go.

Miss Bryan gave my drippy overalls an acid stare. She shot a disapproving look at Louise's still wet skirt. "You two can sit in the same seat and drip on each other," she snorted.

We got back in time for supper in the dining hall.

Afterwards I drifted back to the dorm, got my English book and brought it down to the lounge. I was working on past perfects when someone shouted "Blackjack" in a back corner.

I walked over to where Troy, Red, and a couple of other guys were bent over a card table, playing Blackjack for a nickel a game.

"Want in, 'Fesser?" Troy asked.

"I'll jist watch for a few minutes."

Catching on to the game was easy. Troy, the dealer, dealt each player a card, face down. One by one, the players bet that the card dealt plus one or more would beat the dealer's hand. An ace counted one or eleven; a king, queen, or jack, ten; all other cards were counted at face value. An ace and a picture card made a perfect score, 21. Over 21, the player "busted."

Georgie came strolling up. "Deal me in. I feel lucky tonight."

Troy looked at me questioningly. "You want in now, 'Fesser?"

"I'm broke," I confessed.

Troy pitched me five nickels. "Pay me back when your Mama sends you some money. Or if you win big tonight."

Troy dealt the cards for a new round. I got an ace. Glory be! My next card was a jack of spades. I hollered "Blackjack" and swept up my winnings.

I won four straight rounds, then lost a couple. By ten o'clock I'd paid Troy back and had a pile of nickels in front of me. A whole dollar's worth.

"'Fesser, you lucky dog," exclaimed Georgie.

"You're a real Blackjack."

By eleven o'clock I had a dollar and a half. By midnight my pile was even bigger. Now all the players were calling me "Blackjack."

"I'm out," Red said. "Gotta get some sleep if I'm gonna wake up in time to catch the church bus for Sunday school." Red looked across the table at me. "Ever'body's supposed to go, but I've never seen you on any church bus, 'Fesser. How about goin' with me tomorrow?"

"Nah," I said. "I'll be too sleepy."

Sunday morning I slept until eleven. I showered and dressed, then meandered across the campus lawn toward the eatery. On the way, I caught up with Troy, who invited me to eat with him. We were halfway through when the churchgoers came trooping in, dressed to the gills. Howie had Jeri Lynn in tow. Marie, Emma, and Pansy brought their trays to sit with Troy and me. They saw that neither of us had ties. "Can we eat with you two heathen?" Pansy asked. Troy laughed. I said, "Shore, just don't tell on us.."

After dinner the girls went back to the dorm to change. Troy and I moseyed over to the basketball gym and shot goals, starting out at a nickel for the first guy who, taking turns, could drop the ball through the hoop five times. Before long, three other guys were out on the court, wagering with us.

I ended up with a dollar and a half. "Blackjack, y'ar a crack shot," Troy said. "You oughta go out for the basketball team."

"Oh, I am. Next month, when Coach Tucker starts practice."

Sunday evening I played Blackjack again. Same for Monday, Tuesday, Wednesday, Thursday, and Friday nights. It didn't hurt my luck that I was too young to drink with my opponents. Drinking made them reckless. Coming into the wee hours of Saturday morning, I had over 20 dollars in my pocket.

Every time I won, Red would say, "You lucky dog!" And Georgie would pipe, "'Fesser, you're a real Blackjack."

The new moniker stuck. Fewer and fewer people called me "'Fesser" anymore. In the dorm, gym, dining hall, classroom, and everywhere else on campus I was "Blackjack." Even Mr. Tommy, after he heard others addressing me by that name, started calling me "Blackjack."

Then came the really big gamble. I was determined to make the Tech basketball team. My friends tried to tell me I didn't have a chance, that I was too young, too short and too skinny. That was true, but I could outrun them all, I never seemed to get winded and I could shoot baskets with the best of them.

"Blackjack, the big boys will stomp on you like an ant," Georgie said. I wanted to tell him, "Ole Carrot-top, I've got a better chance of making the basketball squad than you have in football."

The fall term ended in early November. My grades were better than before, though certainly not the greatest. Mr. Rollow and Coach Fiser each gave me a D. I protested to both. Mr. Rollow said, "I'm sorry, son, but a D is all you deserve." I reminded Coach Fiser that I had run the four-mile race in less time than half of the other boys. "Yeah," he conceded, "but you didn't follow my instructions. And you didn't do well enough in calisthenics."

DuLaney and Merrill gave me Cs, and I got a big B from Miss Clark — bless her dear soul. "Hefley," she said on the last day, "if you were a female, you'd make a good secretary."

A day after I got my report card, I got a letter from Daddy (who rarely wrote to anybody), saying I had a new brother they'd named John Paul. "I'll meet you at Lurton on Saturday," he said.

Daddy was there with bells on when the Red Ball rolled up to Sutton's Store. He trotted over to get my bag.

"Shore been missin' ya, son. C'mon and let's git goin'. Yer Mama's waitin' at the store. I told her to close up and get a little rest, but she's afraid of missing a few customers."

"She's workin' in the store with a week-old baby?"

"Yep, bein' it's Saturday, air big tradin' day. Yer twin sisters air takin' care of little Johnny, an' Monk is helpin' his mama wait on the trade."

Johnny was asleep in a little home-made cradle when I rushed in. My nine-year-old twin sisters were hovering over him. The two younger girls, Freddie and Jimmie, were playing jacks in a window well. Mama was waiting on a customer. Monk was toting a 25-pound sack of salt out to a wagon.

Mama stopped only long enough to give me a hug and went right back to packing groceries in a flour sack for Walter Coonts. Not until after supper, which she cooked, did she start asking me questions about school. Mainly, she wanted to know if I had gotten homesick living in the dorm, and if my grades were any better.

"Well, I've been pretty busy," I said, thinking it better not to mention the almost nightly Blackjack games in the dorm lounge. "I'm doin' better in my classes. Got a B and two Cs." I didn't mention the two Ds. She could see them when my report card came in the mail.

The week-end zipped by. When it was time to go, I promised my baby brother, "When you get big enough to wade the creek, I'll come home and take ya fishin'."

Back at Tech I enrolled for my winter quarter classes: Phys Ed, Zoology, Chemistry, Survey of Math, Advanced Typing, and Old Testament. My roomie said the Bible course, as taught by Reverend Fritz Goodbar, the pastor of the First Baptist Church, would be a breeze. "But watch out for ole Truman McEver in General Chemistry. Those who have had him say he's rough as a cob."

Talk on campus was all about resuming varsity basketball. The sport had been dropped after the war started, but the powers that be were expecting Tojo and Hitler to be vanquished within a few months. So why not get an early start with basketball? President Hull and representatives of eight other Arkansas colleges met in Little Rock and so agreed.

The students went wild when Mr. Hull announced this at Wednesday assembly. Coach John Tucker said he'd be at the gym at four p.m. to meet boys wanting to try out for the Wonder Boys' squad.

Not having a three o'clock class, I was at the gym an hour early, shooting goals and dribbling the ball inside and outside of my legs. By three-thirty, 13 other hopefuls were on the floor, including Howie Parish and my two Judy high school classmates, C.B. Hudson and Junior Johnson.

Coach Tucker, who had seen me shooting free throws in the gym, took everybody's name and began running drills on both ends of the court. I kept listening for my name, but he never called it. When the practice was over, he called me over.

"Hefley, mah boy," he said, patting me on the head as if I were his little pet dog. "If you were two or three years older, I'd consider you in a minute. For one thing, you're good at the free throw line."

I thought he might have seen my grades, or heard about my Blackjack exploits in the dormitory.I blinked back tears. " 'Cause I'm not old enough — that's the only reason?"

"Son, that's not the only reason. Little and skinny as you are, I can't take the chance of you getting hurt."

A couple of weeks later I came upon the empty Tech bus parked in front of Wilson Hall. In a half hour the Wonder Boys would be leaving to play Hendrix Methodist College in Conway, about 50 miles from Tech. I sneaked on the bus and squirmed into a little alcove behind the back seat.

The team began boarding a few minutes later. Coach Tucker took a seat in front beside the bus driver.

Howie Parish moved to the back and saw my hand clutching the top of the seat where I was hiding. "What — who's that?" He stood up to see better. "'Hefley — Blackjack! What are you doin' on the bus?"

Fortunately, the roar of the motor drowned out

our voices. "Shhh," I whispered. "Don't tell anybody I'm back here."

About 25 miles down the highway I emerged from my hiding place. Howie's voice echoed through the bus: "Blackjack's here. We're gonna be lucky tonight."

Coach Tucker did not think my presence was funny at all. He threatened to put me off the bus and make me walk back. Some of the players urged him to let me go on with the team. He grumbled, "I'll think about it."

I didn't say a word, just tried to look pitiful. Coach must have felt sorry for me, for when we stopped to eat at a cafe in Morrilton he handed me a meal ticket. But when we took our places in the Hendrix gym, he ordered, "'Fesser, Blackjack, whatever they call you, you sit right here beside me, and don't move 'til we're ready to go home."

When C.B. made two points, I jumped up and hollered, "Pour it on! Pour it on!" Coach Tucker reached out to pull me back down, then dropped his arm. "Aw, son," he said, "I reckon you can cheer."

I whooped and hollered and screamed every time a Wonder Boy made a goal. All the while I was trying to figure how I could make money on the games. I couldn't bet against our team — maybe I could take bets based on the point spread.

The Wonder Boys won the game 35 to 30. "You should have let me play," I told the coach on the way home. "The score would have been 50 to 30."

As for hiding on the bus, Coach Tucker said if I did it again, he'd order me to be in my room by seven o'clock every night for two weeks.

Chapter 13

"Science, the Bible and Dancing"

Zoology, under Mr. Tommy, started Wednesday morning at eight.

As usual, Mr. Tommy took his time in lighting up before getting into the subject.

"How many of you have been to a big city zoo?" he finally asked.

Most of us hadn't. Georgie raised his hand high. "I've been to the Little Rock Zoo a zillion times."

Howie couldn't hold himself back. "You look like a zoo animal."

Georgie shouted back, "Takes one to know one."

Mr. Tommy raised his hands. "Boys, boys! The point I'm wanting to make is that there are nearly as many branches of zoology as there are life forms in, well, the Little Rock Zoo. Who can name and define the five divisions of zoology?"

Pansy was faster on the draw than Howie. "Entomology is the study of bugs. Ornithology deals with birds. Embryology studies the development from an egg to a fully formed person or animal…"

"Yeah," Howie interrupted, "and genetics is the

science of heredity, and — "

Mr. Tommy stopped Howie in mid-sentence. "All of you should have learned that and more in high school. Now I'm gonna give each of you a branch to study and report back to us next class period. Some of you may even decide to take one of these divisions as your profession."

Georgie had to open his mouth: "Entomology sounds interesting to me."

"It would," Howie responded. "I've had you figured as a little buggy."

"Just for that, you're not gonna ride in my convertible again," Georgie snapped.

Mr. Tommy held up his hands again. "Boys, boys, stop it, or I'll send you both to the zoo."

I stayed awake in Mr. Tommy's zoology, but I had trouble keeping my eyes open in the class that followed, General Chemistry.

I'd been forewarned about Mr. Truman McEver. Ernie McElven, a sophomore from Morrilton, had told me the day before, "Mr. Mac is tougher than Miss Massie. Not as sarcastic, but tougher. If you don't do the work, he'll flunk you in the bat of an eye."

Mr. Mac, a slim, sandy-haired ex-basketball coach, let us have it on the first day. "In my class, you will sit up straight, pay attention and address me as 'sir.' If you cooperate, study and apply yourself, I'll give you a good grade. If you don't, your grade will be less — an F, if you deserve it."

His eyes bore into me as if he knew about my pitiful scholastic record. "Some of you may have made less than ideal grades up to this time. If that's the case, it isn't too late to straighten up and fly right. If you aspire to be a doctor and do well under me, I'll recommend you to medical school. I take great pride in saying that all of my pre-med students, except one, are in medical school or practicing medicine today.

"It's up to you. Your life will be what you make of it."

With that he launched into a long introduction on the subject at hand. "Chemistry seeks to discover what things are made of and how they can change. A piece of material may get cooler or warmer, softer or harder, change color, change from a solid to a liquid, or even a gas and still remain the same substance. That's chemistry at work. . ."

ZZzzzzzz. ZZzzzzzz. The sleep I'd lost playing Blackjack the night before was catching up with me. ZZzzzzzz. Zzzzzzzz.

Plunk! A hard object suddenly hit my forehead, straight between my eyes. My eyes flew open as a piece of chalk tumbled off my collar. Mr. Mac went right on lecturing as if nothing had happened. Nobody fell asleep during the rest of that class period.

After dinner, I stayed awake in Miss Clark's Advanced Typing and Mr. Roy Weedin's Survey of Math. I could type and figure and as demonstrated the next day, I knew a little about Bible history.

I'd never been a Sunday school boy, but I had heard the old-timers argue the Bible on our store porch for hours on end. And I did have an old Bible story book that had been passed down through our family. I used that as my text instead of the Bible.

Jumping Jack was right. On his first exam, Reverend Goodbar asked very simple questions: "Who tempted Eve?" "Who was the oldest man who ever lived?" "Name the first ship captain mentioned in the Bible."

For the next test, he gave us a list of ten Bible characters and asked us to write a paragraph about what each one did. Then he had us adapt one character's exploits to a modern situation. Mr. Goodbar liked Troy Morrison's adaptation so much that he asked him to read it in class.

"The commander-in-chief called ole Moses up to headquarters and gave him orders to go behind enemy lines and rescue the Jews from the Egyptians. When Moses and his people got to the Red Sea, God told Moses to march his people into the sea. Moses balked, saying, 'They'll all drown.' But the Commander said, 'Just obey my orders. I'll take care of them.'

"Well, ole Moses hollered, 'Forward march!' the Commander rolled back the waters, and they all marched over on dry land.

"Now after they had crossed over and the water had rolled back over their path, they looked back and saw the Egyptians building a pontoon bridge for their tanks to cross over on. Moses ran up to the Jewish radio shack and called up a squadron of B-29 bombers to blow up the bridge. When the bridge was destroyed, the Egyptians marched into the Red Sea and they all drowned."

Everybody I talked to made an A in Old

Testament for the winter term.

The big social to-do that term was the Sadie Hawkins Day dance. Participants dressed up as characters from the Li'l Abner comic strip. I loaned one of my pairs of overalls to Jumping Jack. We and at least ten other boys dressed up as Li'l Abner. For the first time since I got to Tech, I felt appropriately dressed.

When I told Georgie that his hair was the wrong color, he stretched an old mop over his carrot-top. Marie and Jeri Lynn were among at least 10 "Daisy Maes." Emma was one of the Mammy's complete with corn cob pipe. Howie and a couple of other boys came as Pappy. Troy Morrison took the role of Lonesome Polecat. Troy's roommate came as Hairless Joe. Pansy masqueraded as Tobacco Rhoda.

The fun started that afternoon on the athletic field where the girls competed to "catch" a date for the evening dance. Heavily outnumbered, the boys lined up about 50 yards ahead of the girls on the running track. Miss Bryan gave the signal. Coach Fiser blew his whistle. The chase was on.

Jeri Lynn and a dozen other girls began chasing Howie. He ran around the track a couple of times before pretending to stumble in front of Jeri Lynn. When she grabbed him, the girl behind her screamed, "Foul!"

Howie was the exception. The rest of us boys led the girls a merry chase.

Marie, Pansy and three other girls ran screaming after a new boy from Fort Smith. Another girl jumped in from the side and tackled him around the knees. Marie started after me. I caught the south football goal post where two more boys were already roosting.

Marie grabbed my foot, yelling, "You're goin' to the dance with me."

I pulled free and shinnied up to the crossbar. "Yah, yah, I ain't goin' to the dance with you."

Marie started after another boy. He easily outran her.

Georgie came flying by, his mop-head streaming in the breeze. Marie grabbed his belt and held on. "You're my date for tonight," she shouted. She had him.

To my great relief, not a single girl caught me that afternoon. I didn't want to go to the ole dance anyway.

All my gambling buddies went to the dance. I fell asleep around 11 o'clock listening to the radio. Sometime after midnight Jumping Jack woke me from a sound snooze. Jack was assigned to handle the music for the dance, so I knew he'd be coming home late.

He didn't bother to be quiet. "All right," I mumbled sleepily, "who won?"

"George Moore was voted best-dressed boy. He came as Lonesome Polecat. Carla Young, one of the Daisy Maes, won the girls' crown."

From force of habit, Jack flipped on a record. I threw a shoe at him.

"Sorry," he said. "Why are you in bed so early?"

" 'Cause, I couldn't find anybody to play Blackjack with me."

I really felt like a misfit. The biggest social activity was dancing, an activity for which I had little interest and no talent. With the gender imbalance the way it was, the girls had to do most of the asking.

"'Fesser," Marie whispered in my ear one afternoon as we were leaving Mr. DuLaney's class, "you know, you're kinda cute. How about takin' me to the Christmas dance?"

A giggle spilled out of my throat. "You know I ain't no dancer."

" 'Fesser" — she never called me "Blackjack" — college isn't college unless you learn how to dance. Let's go get a coke."

I never did say a straight-out no to taking Marie to the dance. I didn't want to hurt her feelings.

We were sipping our cokes in the Techionery, when I reminded Marie of the time I had tripped over Pansy's feet. "Remember how upset she was with me?"

"Yeah," Marie grimaced, "but she doesn't have my touch."

There were only a couple of other people in the place. Marie slid out of the booth, pulled me up, and shoved a nickel in the juke box for Les Brown's "I've Got My Love To Keep Me Warm."

Placing her hand in the small of my skinny back, she eased me around the floor to the rhythm of the popular song. "Watch my feet; follow me," she instructed. Following her directions, I thought that for a beginner I did pretty well. In a rush of holiday good will, I agreed to take her.

I still had only one going-out suit, the $8.98 tweed

Sears & Roebuck special. I'd done some growing since graduation, and it fit quite snuggly with my ankles hanging out. I still hadn't learned how to tie a tie, so I wore a clip-on. Jumping Jack wasn't around to look me over. He was long gone to the Armory to check out the sound system.

Marie — wearing a satiny, shimmering blue evening gown — and a boodle of other girls, were waiting in Caraway's fancy lobby for their dates when I walked in. "Hey, look at Blackjack, er 'Fesser," giggled Emma. "Don't he look grand?"

"Doesn't he look grand?" came the correction from Mr. Tommy's beau, Miss Bryan, seated close to a girl talking on the telephone.

Marie caught my arm and we hurried out. "That Miss Bryan can be intimidating," she muttered. "Did you notice how close she hung to the phone. She wants to hear everything we're saying."

My date was in a mood for gab. "You know what she told a bunch of us a few minutes ago? 'Young ladies, when you're dancing with your date, keep your mind above his belt.' We were horrified."

I could feel my face redden. "Oh, 'Fesser, I'm sorry," Marie giggled. "I shouldn't have repeated that. I didn't mean anything." I looked up at her and saw that her face was flaming too.

The rhythmic clicking of Marie's high heels accompanied us as we swept down El Paso Avenue a short ways and crossed to the Armory. As we entered through the streamer bedecked door, she kept her arm tucked behind my pointy left elbow, smiling as if she had caught the prize of the season. Once inside she leaned down and brushed her lips against my ear, not to whisper a sweet nothing, but to say, "Remember, watch my feet, 'Fesser. Move with me."

Voices emanated from our left where some of my so-called friends were lined up looking me over. "Hey, look at Blackjack and Marie. Look how he's all duded up."

Josh caught my eye. "Hey, why didn't ya wear yer overalls, Blackjack?"

"Why don'tcha go back to the barn?" I shot back.

Marie ignored the calls. "C'mon, Blackjack." That was the first time she had called me by my new nickname. "A one, a two..." Mr. Williamson's band struck up a tune by Irving Berlin. Marie snaked a perfumed left arm around my neck, holding my body straight with her right hand. A touch of nausea rose in my stomach. I kept my eyes glued on Marie's feet.

"You're doing good, Blackjack," she whispered. "Just stay with me."

Then Marie made the mistake of circling back to where my friends were parked. I heard Joshua snicker, along with Troy Morrison. Then Georgie came dancing by like a professional. "Blackjack, hold your gal tighter. Careful. Don't step on her toes."

"C'mon, 'Fesser, Blackjack," Marie encouraged. "Just watch me. One, two, three. You can do it, boy. C'mon. Hey! Ouch! You stepped on my foot."

I could feel eyes centered on us. Two couples had completely stopped and were staring at us. The snickers from around the room had turned to all-out laughter. The catcalls and whistles kept coming from all directions.

"C'mon, Blackjack. Let's swing over to the other side. Get away from these dummies who are makin' you nervous.

"Okay. One, two, three. C'mon, keep movin' with me. Ouch! Ouch! Ouch! Oh, Blackjack, you're impossible — maybe we'd better rest awhile."

We found two empty chairs near the wall, close to the front door. I had had it. When Marie turned her head to talk to Emma, I lammed for the door. The last I heard was Josh calling, "Where ya goin', Blackjack? Come on back, boy. The dance is jist gettin' started."

I ran rull tilt toward the dorm. I didn't look back until I reached the door of Wilson Hall. I later heard that Marie had found a free cadet and danced with him for the rest of the evening. When asked about me, she said, "I don't know that little savage."

She never asked me to another dance.

Chapter 14

"Jackpot Charley"

My winter term grades could have been better. On the other hand, as I explained to Mama during the break, they could have been worse. Much worse. Besides the A in Old Testament, I got Bs in Advanced Typewriting and Survey of Math, a C in Phys Ed, but Ds in Mr. Mac's Chemistry and Mr. Tommy's Zoology.

Mr. Tommy's D grade really hurt. I told him so. He said, "'Fesser, mah boy, you didn't turn in your assignments when they were due. You spent too much time playin' cards and messin' around. Accordin' to my sources, you've been shufflin' the deck 'til past midnight, four and five nights a week. They don't call you Blackjack for nothing. Gambling and good grades don't mix."

Shoulders drooping, I slunk out like a whipped puppy. If Miss Massie had talked to me like that it would have made me mad. A scolding from kind and gentle Mr. Tommy made me feel guilty for letting down such a good man.

Tech would be changing from a term to a

semester schedule. If I didn't enroll after the mid-winter break, I would be out for four-and-a-half months. That was something to think about during break time, even though I would not be 15 until June.

I was tired of college. Tired of trying to act grownup and always being with people who were older. I told my parents. With two Ds in science courses, Mama now knew I would never make it into medical school. As for dropping out of Tech again, Mama said, "It's up to you. If you want to stay home a while and go back for the fall semester, we can certainly use you in the store. With the big market for roots, fur hides, and stave bolts, people have more money to spend now. And you'll get more business experience."

I was running hot and cold about Tech when a wholesale gambling catalog came in the mail addressed to the store. "We get the candy punchboards from this company," Mama explained.

The candy punchboards were peanuts compared to other merchandise offered by the gambling company. I thumbed through page after page of pictures of money boards — from a penny to a dollar a punch. I looked longingly at money-making slot machines; roulette wheels; Blackjack, crap, and poker tables, the works. If the catalog said gambling was legal only in Nevada, I never noticed. I was too caught up with the dream of making thousands of easy dollars to care about legality. Why, by the time I was old enough to drive, I might have enough to buy a new convertible, like Georgie. I would pack my dream car full of girls and cruise down El Paso

Avenue. The teachers who had given me low grades would gawk and say, "There goes ole Blackjack. I had him in my class."

"I'm not goin' back to Tech," I informed Mama. "I'm gonna stay home and make some moolah. I can get me a slot machine for only $32.95."

"Well, now, I don't know, James Carl. I don't want you gettin' yerself in debt."

"Aw, Mama, I won't. I'll make big bucks. I know I will. I could even help pay my college bills."

"Order only what you think you can pay for," Mamas said. I picked out the small, nickel slot machine that was only 18 inches high. It didn't have automatic pay off, but it was a beginning. Then I chose a thousand-punch "Jackpot Charley." At two bits a punch I'd take in $250 buckeroos and pay out $200 in cash prizes. Less $10 for the gambling wholesaler's bill, I'd make $40.

Cousin Noel Martin, the North Mail carrier, delivered Jackpot Charley and the slot machine on a Thursday. I wanted to set them out for business right away. "Wait until Saturday," Mama decreed, "when there'll be a much bigger crowd."

Mama didn't say I couldn't advertise. I told everybody in town that come Saturday, they'd have the opportunity to win from $5 to $25 for a measly two bits a punch, plus getting to try out the very first slot machine in the county. I didn't mention that I was guaranteed a 20 percent profit on the slot.

Saturday morning I popped out of bed before daylight, waking everybody in the house. Mama fixed an early breakfast while Daddy fed his coon hounds. By sunup, our general store was open for Saturday business. I propped the first money punchboard ever seen in Judy on top of the big glass case, and positioned the slot machine near the cash register. I was ready for customers.

Cousin Lonzo came bumbling in, packing a sack of slippery-elm bark on his back. Lonzo was just one of many hill farmers harvesting roots and barks essential for making medicines that would save the lives of wounded soldiers. Mama was the purchasing agent and Daddy delivered the products to a pharmaceutical company representative in Harrison.

Lonzo plopped his sack of elm bark down on our big feed scale.

"How much, Hester?"

Mama noted the weight. "Comes to two dollars and thirteen cents." She handed Lonzo eight quarters, two nickels, and three pennies. I'd already asked Mama to give quarters and nickels in change. "That'll make it easier for them to try ole Jackpot Charlie and the slot."

I shoved Charlie under Lonzo's eyes. "Quarter a punch and you get paid off in cash."

"How much can I win?" Lonzo wanted to know.

"From $5 to $25. Try a punch."

Lonzo pitched me a quarter. I handed him the puncher. Lonzo drew back his arm and pushed out a tiny slip of paper.

"I got number, uh, 200." His eyes swept over the list of winners. "Well, whoopy-do-da. I win ten bucks on the first punch."

He reached out a big paw. "Pay me, James Carl."

I had to borrow the money from Mama's cash register. "That board had better not have all winners," Mama mumbled nervously as she counted out five one dollar bills and twenty quarters.

Uncle Maynard came rushing in. "I heerd you got a money punchboard, 'Fesser. Let me try mah luck."

On the second punch he hit a $20 winner. "Hey, hey, hey," he cackled. "I'm goin' home and show this to mah ole lady."

Mama was really looking pale.

The customers went wild. Lonzo and Charlie Johnson almost got into a fist fight over the puncher. I grabbed it up and ordered, "Take turnabout. One of you can try the slot machine." Boy, did I feel important.

They punched ole Charley out before sundown. Lonzo lost every quarter he had. I made my $50 in profit, less the $10 cost of the board. I hadn't had to pay out anything from the slot machine, but didn't know how many nickels it had eaten. Mama was ecstatic. If there'd been a phone in Judy, I would have called Mr. Roy Weedin, the business professor at Tech, to tell him about my good fortune.

With Mama's permission, I ordered three more Charleys, plus a nickel, a dime, and a dollar punchboard. By February, I was making almost as much money on a Saturday as Mama was in the store. I bought new clothes, which I really needed because I was finally starting to get taller. I also bought two new fishing reels and rods, a box of lures, and a portable Smith Corona typewriter.

Things were going great in my little world, but

the news from the outside was more dramatic. The deadliest war in human history was now moving toward a climax. General MacArthur was fast liberating the Philippines. American B-29 bombers were pulverizing Japanese cities while thousands of American boys were dying on Iwo Jima. One was Wilson Strong, my former school teacher, Clara Kent's nephew. He and I had played marbles together in Judy.

Victory in Europe was near at hand. The Big Three — Roosevelt, Churchill, and "Uncle" Joe Stalin — met at Yalta and divided post-war Europe into "spheres of influence."

Night after night, commentator Gabriel Heatter told us, "There's good news tonight." The Rising Sun was sinking. The handwriting for Hitler was on the wall.

During that exciting spring of 1945, nobody ever told Mama or me that I was breaking the law. Not Uncle Loma, the town constable. He stayed busy corralling drunks and breaking up fights. Nor Sheriff Russell Burdine, who roved the hills and hollows tracking down illegal moonshine stills.

Sunday through Friday, I went fishing — usually with David Criner. Day after day we perched on the ledge of the Tom Greenhaw bluff, our fishing lines dangling in the cool, green water. We didn't hook many fish, but we did a lot of speculating on the progress of the war and other world events. I also shared Tech stories and nagged at David to enroll for the fall semester. David's rejoinder was, "If you like Tech so well, why aren't you down there now?"

"I'm goin' back," I always said. "I'm goin' back."

Saturday continued to be the big day for my gambling business. I hung over the counter taking money and handing out winnings until the last customer left. Then I joined the horseshoe pitching gang in front of Johnson's cobblestone house, located directly across the street from our store. I might have been little and skinny, but I was the best horseshoe pitcher in town. After supper came the weekly western movie in a tent some outsider pitched beside Nichol's cafe. The Grand Ole Opry followed the movie, keeping me up until midnight. I lived for Saturdays.

My Tom Sawyerish life got to be boring on occasion and there were times when I did wish to be back at Tech, listening to Mr. DuLaney pontificate on world events, hearing Mr. Tommy discuss the life of a grasshopper, even listening to Jumping Jack's music.

Then one warm Saturday afternoon in March, my punchboard crowd began slipping out the front door. Mama peeped out a window and saw a strange car parked across the street in front of the cobble-stoned house which Junior Johnson's parents had vacated to move to Springfield, MO. I tucked my gambling paraphernalia in a drawer behind the counter and stepped out on the porch to see for myself.

A middle-aged couple brushed past me, on their way into the store. Looking up the street, I saw about 50 men and boys following two giggling teenage girls, a short one and a tall one, both decked out in white shorts. No female, to my remembrance, had ever appeared in Judy wearing such skimpy attire.

Cousin Clyde Hefley — about my age — came

racing around the corner of our store. "Whar's them nekkid girls?"

I pointed toward the cafe. He started running up the street.

A commanding female voice with a clipped, northern accent came from behind me. "Rosemary? Treela?" It was the woman I had seen going into our store. The girls turned and strolled back toward the Johnson house, with their entourage following.

Mama was standing on the store porch watching and frowning at the girls. "Who are these people?" I asked Mama.

"Mr. and Mrs. Brandt from Delavan, Illinois. They're good friends of the missionary women from Hasty, Florence Billings and Marie Olsen."

I'd seen the northern missionary women a few times when they came and spoke to the students at Judy School.

"The Brandts have been staying at Hasty. They've rented the Johnson house," Mama reported.

The newcomers with their strange northern accent moved in the next week. It happened that only the short one, Rosemary, barely 13, belonged to Hazel and Pete Brandt. The tall girl was their niece, Treela, who was just visiting.

When the Brandts came to stock up on groceries from our store. I boldly introduced myself to Rosemary, informing her that I was a student at Arkansas Tech.

"You don't look old enough to be in college," she giggled.

"Aw, I'm almost 15."

I could tell by the sparkle in her eyes that she was impressed.

I figured Rosemary's parents had taken a shine to me when Mrs. Brandt said, "We're having a Bible study at our house on Sunday evening. Would you like to come?"

I didn't know that she was going around inviting everybody in Judy. Not many grown-ups showed up, but a passel of boys were there, maneuvering to get close to Rosemary and Treela. Mrs. Brandt finally had to calm them down so Marie Olsen, one of the Hasty missionaries, could lead the study.

The novelty of the newcomers wore off. When it became known that the Brandts were Baptists, most of the crowd didn't come back. Anxious to get into Rosemary's best graces, I informed her, "One of my best buddies at Tech is a Baptist." I didn't mention that Ole Red was a gambling pal.

Tuesday, April 10. The sky blackened in the morning and poured out a deluge during the afternoon. The rain pounded the earth all night and the next morning before slackening off. The creek rose and roared. Fallen trees blocked the roads and knocked down power poles, breaking wires and silencing radios dependent upon electricity.

By Thursday noon the air was cool, the sky a brilliant blue. One of Mama's cousins, who lived in a high mountain cove, came in our store looking for some aspirin. "Fer mah womern," he said. "She's got a mean headache."

He looked around the circle of men lazing beside the pot-bellied stove. "You fellers don't look sad at all."

"Naw, we're jist glad the rain is over," Daddy noted. "We're waitin' now for the powerline workers to get across the creek and give us our electricity back. Our radios have been dead since the first of the week."

"Then you ain't heerd that ole Roosevelt died," Cousin Joel said. "I heerd the news over mah battery radio last night."

We suddenly got real interested in what Cousin Joel was saying. "The President was at his rest house in Warm Springs, Georgie. An artist lady was drawing his pitcher when he fell over in his chair, complainin' of a headache. My womern heard that and her head's been hurtin' ever since. That's why I come fer some aspirin."

I listened with wide eyes, wishing I could be at Tech and hear President Hull, Mr. DuLaney and Mr. Merrill talk in Assembly about the death of America's four-term president and the succession of Vice-president Harry Truman.

The electricity people got the downed power poles back up on Monday. The radio commentators were all saying the war couldn't last much longer. Russian soldiers were now in Berlin. The Japs couldn't hold out much longer on Okinawa. The invasion of Japan was close. So said H.V. Kaltenborn, Walter Winchell, and ole "good news tonight" Gabriel Heatter.

Hitler disappeared from the public eye. News came later that he had married his long-time mistress, Eva Braun, then both had swallowed poison. Seven days later Germany surrendered.

The Japanese lost Iwo Jima and Okinawa, with terrible loss of life for both sides, but still refused to surrender.

July came hot and muggy. Rosemary and I sat on her front porch, exchanging possum grins. Mama was eager for school to start at Judy in August. As much as she loved her school-age kids, she was tired of having them under foot, hollerin' "Mama this" and "Mama that," while she was trying to hang onto little Johnny and wait on a customer at the same time.

I was now pretty much settled on going back to Tech for the fall semester. My punch board business had drizzled off. For one thing, Jeames and Gussie Nichols had boards out in their cafe. Good ole gullible Mama had let them see my gambling catalog. For another, some of my customers had figured out that the operator — me — always won in the end.

Still, there was flirty little Rosemary. "James Carl," she said batting her eyelashes, "you oughta go back to college. You're just wastin' your life fishing and gambling. We can see each other when you come home for visits."

There was the problem of Rosemary's new admirer, my second cousin, Kenneth Hefley. He had been attending the Sunday night Bible study at the Brandts too.

I sat on one side of Rosemary, Kenneth on the other. She'd bat her eyes at him, then turn to me and grin. Having two admirers was fun for her.

I kept thinking of asking her for a Saturday evening date to see the movie in the tent beside

Nichols' cafe, but was afraid she'd turn me down. Then one Wednesday night, I spotted Kenneth headed for her front porch where she was seated on the swing. I ran to catch up with him.

We both spoke at the same time: "How 'bout goin' to the movie with me Saturday night?"

Rosemary was both pleased and puzzled. Her eyes swept over Kenneth, then back to me.

An inspiration hit me. "Let's pitch a horseshoe game," I proposed to Kenneth, "to see who gets to take her."

Kenneth accepted. I won and took her the first time. He won the next week and got the pleasure of escorting her to the movie tent.

I was having second thoughts about going back to Tech, when Kenneth got a job in Little Rock. I took her three Saturday nights in a row, then he came home for a weekend and we both took her.

Kenneth returned to Little Rock. The weather heated up. The creek ran dry at many places. Fishing ran from poor to miserable. News came from Europe of horrible monstrosities perpetrated upon millions of Jews by the Nazi barbarians. Japan was still refusing to surrender.

Those who had their radios on were electrified when the president announced that a United States plane, code-named "Little Boy," had dropped an atomic bomb on Hiroshima, Japan, killing tens of thousands of people. "If they [the Japanese] do not now accept our terms they may expect a rain of ruin from the air, the like of which has never been seen on earth," President Truman said.

We kept the radio on in our store. I left my punchboards untended to hover before the speaker, ears tensed for the next news break-in.

Two days later the flash came that a second devastating atomic bomb, called "Fat Man," had been dropped on the major military port of Nagasaki.

The Japanese finally called it quits.

That night when Mama was closing the store, Daddy mentioned that he'd be making a trip the next day to Mr. Nebo at Russellville, to buy a load of watermelons. "You wanna go with me, Son?" he asked.

He looked over at Cousin Lonzo, who was waiting for an invitation from Mama to eat supper with us. "Got room fer you, Lonz," Daddy said.

The three of us left at four the next morning, headed south on the familiar road to Russellville. The sun was coming up when we passed the Tech Red Barn. I spotted Josh Brown in the barnyard driving a balky cow toward a milking stall. I hollered at him, but he apparently didn't hear me.

We rolled down El Paso Avenue, past the flag fluttering in front of Wilson Hall. I spotted Georgie's convertible with the top rolled up, parked in its usual place.

Daddy followed the same road the Tech bus had taken in carrying students to Skyview Park for the wiener roast the previous summer. Part way up, he turned off on a rutted farm road and rolled to a stop before a chalk white farm house. We were welcomed by the same watermelon grower I had waved to from the window of the Tech bus the year before.

The farmer rode with us to his big ten-acre patch.

Daddy laid down his instructions to me and Lonzo. "Help us load up first, boys, then you can eat all you want." After Lonzo and I gorged ourselves, the farmer pointed us to his outhouse with a quarter moon on the door.

Necessities cared for, we climbed back in Daddy's truck. Passing through Tech, I spotted Coach Tucker, Mr. Merrill and Mr. Fiser on the field with the football boys, who included Howie and Georgie.

"Slow down, stop a minute," I told Daddy. I jumped out and ran to where Georgie was squatting on the sideline. He jumped up and slapped me on the shoulder. "Blackjack, we've been missin' ya."

Howie came trotting over to shake my hand. "You comin' back this semester?"

My mind was made up. "I'm comin' back. How's the football season look?"

Howie tossed me a confident grin. "Coach Tucker says we're gonna win the state title. Mr. Merrill is our line coach. Coach Fiser is in charge of the backfield. We've got a bunch of boys that wanna play ball." He pointed to Number 87 who was running pass plays. "That's Aubrey Fowler. Played for Tech before the war and now he's come back to his old alma mater. Ever'body calls him 'Cobb.' Ole Ephod, er Coach, says Cobb's a shoo-in for All State."

Daddy began honking. "C'mon, Son, let's go," he hollered.

I slapped Howie on the shoulder. "See ya in a couple of weeks."

Chapter 15

"A Gambling Man"

Lum Hudson, C.B.'s dad, was in our store talking to Mama. "Hester, James Carl can ride with me when I take C.B. back to Tech on Monday."

Mama thought she and Daddy should go, but I assured her, "I'm a big boy now."

Lum, C.B. and I left at five o'clock in the morning to be on time for registration. Junior Johnson was already there.

C.B. and I were in line by nine o'clock. The halls of Ole Main were crowded with students; most of the newcomers were war veterans coming under the GI Bill of Rights.

My eyes swept the lines for familiar faces. There was Marie standing on the first flight of stairs, gabbing with three boys I presumed to be vets. "Hold my place in line," I told C.B.

She greeted me with a handshake. "'Fesser—Blackjack, meet my friends."

I shook hands, making the remark that Marie was a good dancer.

"As long as I'm not dancing with this

bumble-foot," she laughed.

She saw my face color. "Aw, 'Fesser, you're not all that bad."

"How 'bout us eatin' dinner together?" I asked.

"Sorry," she said. "I'm booked for both dinner and supper. With the war over, you've got plenty of competition."

I spoke quickly. "I've got a girl friend at home." With that, I hurried to reclaim my place in line.

Everything ran smoothly until Dean Turrentine's secretary couldn't find my record in the sophomore file. "You say you started to Tech in March, 1944, when we were on the term system? That was almost two years ago."

"Yeah," I said, "but I skipped in and out. Goin' home for a while, then comin' back for a while." I dropped my voice so students nearby couldn't hear. "I also made some bad grades."

"Oh," she grunted, as she began flipping cards in the freshman file. "Here, you are. Hey, now I remember. You enrolled when you were only 13. The *Arka-Tech* ran a big story on you. People called you 'Fesser."

Out of the corner of my left eye, I caught sight of Georgie. At my call ole Carrot Top came trotting over. "Hi'ya, Blackjack. You've come back."

The dean's secretary was not amused. "'Fesser—Blackjack, whatever your name is, take this card to, uh, I guess, Mr. Weedin, since you're a business major."

On my way down the hall, I caught sight of Mr. DuLaney and Miss Massie. Mr. DuLaney saw me and waved. Miss Massie looked my way once, but her face went blank. Maybe she'd forgotten me.

The dark-haired business prof only vaguely remembered me. He ran his finger down my course record. "You made a B in typing and an A in Old Testament your last time here." He managed a wry grin. You didn't do so well in English and your science classes. You had any business experience?"

"I've been running a punchboard business. Nickel to a dollar punch and I have a small slot machine. Mama let's me work off a counter in our store up in Mt. Judy. Made pretty good money for the first couple of months."

Mr. Weedin's eyes narrowed. "You've been operating a gambling business? Isn't that illegal?"

I shrugged. "Nobody ever told me it was. Sheriff Burdine ain't bothered me. My Uncle Loma is the constable. He didn't say anything."

"Well, the dean's office has cleared you, so we'll work out your course schedule. Just don't bring any gambling equipment into your dorm."

"Oh, no sir. Mama put my stuff behind the counter when I left to come back to Tech."

The line behind me wasn't getting any shorter. Mr. Weedin picked up his pencil. "You'll need the second part of General Chemistry. You made a D the first time. You'll need to bring that grade up.

"Botany under Mr. Tomlinson is also required. And you can take two courses in your major. Will Economics and Algebra be okay?"

"Sure."

"That leaves room for one elective. How about

Latin with Mr. Merrill?"

I wasn't sure I knew what Latin was, but I said, "Sure. I like Mr. Merrill."

Mr. Weedin cleared his throat. "Well, there you have it. Just remember, no gambling in the dorms," he repeated.

With so many war veterans enrolled, Wilson Hall was full. Having stayed home the spring semester, I had been bumped from rooming with Jumping Jack. Instead I was assigned to a room on the second floor of the Rock Dormitory above a storeroom for National Guard military equipment.

Somebody else would have to put up with Jumping Jack's music and dancing. My new roommate was Herman Hatfield, a curly-haired, pre-med major from White River country near the Missouri border. His daddy was a doctor, his mother a nurse. We would have Latin and chemistry together.

He quizzed me about my habits. "You drink?"

"Nope."

"Smoke cigarettes?"

"Nope."

"Cuss?"

"Nope."

"Run around with bad girls?"

"Nope. I've got a girl back in Judy. She has Bible studies at her house."

"Whatta ya want to be in life?"

"Mama set her sights on me bein' a doctor," I told him, "but I'm gonna be a businessman."

"What kind of business?" he wanted to know.

"Gambling. I'm gonna go to Nevada and run a casino. I'll relieve rich doctors and lawyers of their money." This was the first time I had told anyone of my casino ambitions.

"Are you putting me on?"

I pulled a deck of cards from my suitcase. "They don't call me Blackjack fer nuthin'. Wanna play a few hands fer a nickel a shot?"

Herman scowled. "I've got better things to do."

Classes wouldn't start for another day. I wandered over to the Techionery. The juke box was blaring. The room was crowded with swinging couples, singing with Frank Sinatra, "Kiss me once, kiss me twice, and kiss me once again; it's been a long, long time."

Jeri Lynn swept by with a crew-cut, older guy I didn't recognize. She blew me a kiss. "Glad to have yah back, Blackjack."

I drifted down to the football field where Howie Parish and a bunch of guys were running plays. As Howie swept down the field in front of me, a long pass floated toward him from quarterback Jessie Grace. Howie scooped in the pass as if it were a feather and hollered, "How am I doin', Blackjack?"

A vision of Jeri Lynn swinging at the Techionery passed through my mind. I bit my tongue to keep from hollering, "Jeri Lynn's got another boy friend."

That evening at supper Jeri Lynn and Marie sat at a table with ten guys, bantering and exchanging small talk as if each were a special friend. I spotted Howie at the football table, sneaking glances at Jeri Lynn. "Those two gals," I told my new roommate,

Herman, "are incurable."

After supper I meandered over to Red Swanson's room on the second floor of Wilson Hall. "Let's get some guys together for a card game," I proposed.

"Yeah," Red said, "we'll start the new semester off right."

Red and I moved up and down the hall, banging on doors, inviting guys to meet us in the lounge about eight o'clock. I went back to the Rock Dorm and found a couple of vets. Louie was the crew-cut fellow I'd seen dancing with Jeri Lynn in the Techionery. Harry, a big, chunky ex-Seabee, who looked twice my age, limped noticeably. "Had a little run-in with a Jap gunner on Okinawa," he explained.

Harry and Louie brought along two bottles of whiskey which they plopped on our card table in full view of anybody walking in. Red dealt the first hand of Blackjack around our circle. I made the first win with an ace and a ten-spot.

Guys drifted in and out. Some asked to be dealt in. Others just sat and watched. Harry and Louie's bottles were three quarters empty by 11 o'clock. Nobody encouraged me to take a drink.

By midnight only Harry and I were playing. "C'mon, let's go," Louie urged us both. Harry shook his head and mumbled, "Blackjack...shee, deal shee cards."

Louie finally got disgusted and left.

By around three a.m., I had won every dollar in Harry's billfold and was owed $180. Harry staggered to his feet and frowned down at me. "I'sssh, ah'll pay ya, Blackjack."

"When?" I wanted to know.

"When ma ship shomes in, thash when. Lesh go 'fore ah fall flat uf mah fasssh."

I led Harry back to his room.

His ship never did come in for me.

My room was only two doors down from Harry's. Dawn was streaking through our window when a scream woke me up. I jerked on my pants and roused Herman. Another scream pierced the walls, then another. The noise was coming from Harry's room.

Herman got him calmed down. Harry apologized, then said, "I was havin' a nightmare. I was back on Okinawa. Guys were falling and hollering all around me. A Jap machine gunner hit me in the leg. I fell back on a guy whose skull had been half shot away. Turned out to be a fellow in my squad."

Harry opened a dresser drawer and pulled out a fresh bottle of booze. "This'll calm me down."

Herman grabbed the bottle. "It'll only make you feel worse, Harry."

Herman carried the bottle to the hall bathroom and poured out every drop.

Harry fell back asleep. Half asleep myself, I followed Herman back to our room and flopped on my bed. Herman picked up his shaving kit, saying, "Might as well get ready to eat."

Herman came back from the bathroom and shook me. "Better get a move on, or you'll miss breakfast."

I woke up a full hour later, thinking the dorm was awfully quiet. Then it dawned: everybody's gone to breakfast.

I slapped some greasy stuff on my hair, raked a

comb across my scalp a couple of times, and lit out running. By the time I got to the dining hall, Joe Sidney had shut down the food line. He pointed to the clock on the wall. "You're way too late, Blackjack."

I was also late for my eight o'clock class, General Chemistry 114B, under Mr. Truman McEver. Next to Miss Massie, in my book, Mr. Mac was Tech's toughest teacher. I remembered Josh Brown saying, "'Fesser, the way you study, you were lucky to get a D in his 114A."

"Feet do yer stuff!" I raced down the sidewalk, dodged a couple of cars on El Paso Avenue, and darted up the stairs of Bailey Hall to Mr. Mac's classroom. Mr. Mac heard the door click and whirled his head around. "Well, well, here's little 'Fesser, or is it Blackjack? Next time, favor us by coming a couple of minutes early, you heah?"

I bobbed my head. "Yes, sir, I heah."

Mr. Mac's eyes bored into mine. "'Fesser we were reviewing a little of what you were supposed to have learned in 114A. The subject at hand is alchemy, one of the earliest forms of chemistry. Will you kindly tell us what the alchemists were trying to find."

I said the first thing that popped into my head. "A cure for cancer?"

Mr. Mac made a notation in his grade book and swung his gaze to Howie. "Mr. Parish, please enlighten your friend on the alchemists."

Howie answered in his usual confident tone. "They were looking for the philosopher's stone that would change lead, iron, and other metals into gold."

By asking questions of everyone in the room, Mr. Mac took us up to the discovery of radioactivity in the 1890s. "A radioactive element," he said, "is one that gives off high energy rays and atomic particles. In 1911 the British physicist Ernest Rutherford theorized that a positively charged nucleus was surrounded by negatively charged electrons. Other scientists showed that the nucleus consisted of particles called protons and neutrons. Dr. Rutherford then changed nitrogen to oxygen by sending rays from radium through nitrogen. What do you suppose was the significance of that?"

One of the two girls in the class answered. "This was the first time scientists changed one element into another."

"Very good, Theresa," Mr. Mac declared. "This led to the first controlled nuclear reaction and the building of super bombs. Without those bombs," Mr. Mac opined, "we might still be at war with Japan."

His gaze swept around the room. Every student was awake, except me. Raising his hand, he flicked a piece of chalk and hit me squarely on the cheek. That got my attention. "'Fesser," he snapped, "the whole world could blow up and you wouldn't know it."

My face reddened as the class roared.

Mr. Mac gave us a reading assignment of 40 pages in the textbook and said we'd be working in the lab next week. Looking squarely at me, he laid down his grading rules: "Pay attention in class, complete your assignments, follow my directions with your lab experiments. Do well on tests. Do all that and I guarantee you'll get a good grade. Goof off and do sloppy work, and you'll likely get an F. Now be on your way. I'll see you Friday morning at eight."

I had ten minutes to get to Algebra in Ole Main. Still in a fog from staying up so late the night before, I bumped — literally — into Georgie on the steps of the administration building facing Wilson Hall. We found we were both going to algebra.

"Algebra's fun for me," Georgie glowed. "I like it almost as well as I do football."

"You on Coach Tucker's first team?" I asked.

"Nope, but I will be. Coach says I've improved 200 percent since we started practice." Georgie eyed me with a confident assurance. "It's amazing what you can do when you set your mind to it."

I didn't say a word.

Mr. Roy Weedin, the algebra teacher, started with a little pep talk about how engineers, chemists, physicists and even industrialists use algebra every day to save time and solve problems. He then announced that we'd review some algebraic basics "you should have learned in high school."

He eased over to the chalkboard and wrote $x + 5 = 8$. "So how much is x?" he asked.

"That's easy," Georgie piped from the front row. "$X = 3$."

Mr. Weedin wrote $x + y = 24$ on the board. "If x is 16, how much is y?"

Georgie shot off his mouth again. "Eight."

"Now," Mr. Weedin announced, "we'll get into sets and variables. To describe a set of numbers in algebra you use a capital letter and put the numbers in brackets. Like this."

He wrote on the chalkboard: W = [2, 4, 6, 8.] My eyes blurred. My head dropped on my chest. Unlike Mr. Mac, Mr. Weedin let me sleep until the end of the period when he motioned for the class to slip out quietly.

He gently shook me awake. "Boy, didn't you get any sleep last night?"

I mumbled, "Not much."

"Were you sick?"

"No. I stayed up gambling with one of the older veterans. Won everything he had and left him owing me $180. Then when I finally did get to bed, he woke me up screaming."

Mr. Weedin solemnly shook his head. "Son, Mrs. Clark had you in typing and she assured me that you aren't dumb. Who's paying your school bills?"

"Mama and Daddy pay some. I pay the rest with my gambling winnings."

"And how old are you now?"

"I turned 15 last June."

"Then you're old enough to face the fact that you could get expelled from school for gambling."

I shifted my gaze downward. "I didn't know that."

"Well, you do now. When's your next class?"

"Two o'clock. I've got Latin with Mr. Merrill."

"Well, go back to the dorm and take a nap before you disgrace yourself in his class too."

I grabbed 40 winks and entered Mr. Merrill's classroom, wide awake for Latin. He checked the roll and got down to business.

Latin, he told us, was not a "dead" language, "although it hasn't been in general use since the Middle Ages. Latin is the parent of the Romance languages. Who can name them?"

Georgie was in this class, too, and he answered immediately. "French, Italian, Spanish, Portuguese, and Romanian. If you know Latin," Georgie added, "you're way ahead of most people in linguistics."

Mr. Merrill grinned. "Right, Georgie. Right. You're turning into quite a scholar."

Georgie beamed.

"Many Americans hear Latin spoken every Sunday in their church rituals," Mr. Merrill continued.

"Roman Catholics," Georgie answered, flashing a know-it-all smile.

"Very good, Georgie," Mr. Merrill continued. "Now let's give someone else the opportunity to speak."

Mr. Merrill looked around the room. "Just a few years ago no college student could graduate without studying Latin. Unfortunately, that isn't true any more. Why is knowing Latin so important to education in the west?

"It's the language of much of the world's literature. Many Latin terms are used in science. We use a lot of Latin words in everyday conversation. I'll guarantee you many sailors were glad to step on *terra firma*. What do we mean by *terra firma*? Solid earth, of course. We may say, 'Mr. Jones has a terrace,' meaning he has a raised level of earth.

"If you want to raise your level of knowledge and advance in this world, you'll need Latin.

"Now, let's look at chapter one."

I kept my mouth shut. I wouldn't have known a *terra firma* if I had seen it walking down the street.

I didn't think my chances of passing Latin 103A were good, and after class I told Mr. Merrill so. He laid a big hand on my shoulder. "Hefley," he assured me. "You can do it. I've believed in you since I first laid eyes on your skinny little torso. All you've got to do is apply yourself."

He looked me straight in the eye. "Just keep telling yourself, 'Latin is the key that opens doors to a wealth of learning. If I want to be somebody, I need to know Latin.' "

Problem was, I just couldn't see where Latin, algebra and chemistry would fit into running a casino in Nevada.

Same for botany which met Tuesday, Thursday and Saturday at eight in the morning.

Dear Mr. Tommy, the teacher everybody loved, was in charge. He knew me from Science Survey and Zoology which I'd taken under him. In the first I'd made a C, in the second a D.

Thursday morning, Mr. Tommy got off on the wrong track with me when he said, "Every human being oughta know botany." I wanted to tell him, "I'm a gambling man, and I don't need to know the difference between chloroplasts and cryptograms." I looked out the window most of the time during this first class period.

Mr. Tommy caught up with me after class. "Son, can I have a little chat with you?"

I couldn't tell Mr. Tommy no.

"Son, 'Fesser—I'm not gonna call you Blackjack as most people do. You couldn't be dumb to graduate from high school at 13."

I just stood there twisting before Mr. Tommy's desk.

"I've seen your grade reports from other classes. You've made an F in English. You've made more Ds than Cs. You did make an A in Old Testament. You're not a church boy, how do you account for that?"

"I think everybody who showed up made an A in Reverend Goodbar's Old Testament."

The wrinkles in Mr. Tommy's sun-drenched face widened. "Well, you certainly aren't a candidate for the honor roll."

I hung my head as he ran on. "Son, I know you like to gamble."

"Yeah," I admitted. "That's 'cause I like to make money."

"Is that all there is to life?"

"It beats everything else I know."

"James, this is a state college. We're not supposed to promote any religion in class, but I'm gonna break rank and tell you that the Good Master tried to help people get their priorities straight. In the Gospel of Mark He asked, 'For what shall it profit a man, if he shall gain the whole world, and lose his own soul?' That's chapter 8, verse 36."

I was beginning to get a little riled. "Mr. Tommy, I'm better than a lot of people at this school. I don't drink, cuss, or run around with bad girls." Looking at Mr. Tommy's ever-present roll your own, I had to add, "And I don't smoke either."

Mr. Tommy paused, seemingly at a loss for words. Finally I said, "I've got a class, Mr. Tommy."

The much-respected teacher placed a hand on my dark head. "Go on to your class, Son. I hope you'll give some serious thought to what the Good Master said about wealth."

My next Thursday class was Economics 163, my second class under Mr. Merrill. The biggest man on campus scrawled on the chalkboard:

ECONOMICS: The study of how goods and services get produced and how they are distributed to people.

"By goods and services is meant everything bought and sold," Mr. Merrill said. "Production is the making of goods and services. Distribution is how the goods and services get to the people.

"Every one of us fits in here somewhere. This college produces a service of education for its student customers. A farmer sells his produce at a market where women buy foodstuffs for their tables. A film company rents a movie to theater operators across the country, who sell tickets to people who want to see it."

I had to ask the question: "Where does a gambling casino fit into economics?"

Surely Mr. Merrill knew about my vocational aspirations. Still he spoke in a straightforward way. "Commercial gambling fits somewhere into the economic picture, although I think it's bad for society. But the majority of citizens in Nevada apparently think differently. For those who go there and make their bets, I guess they see gambling as a pleasurable activity. Although I can't imagine getting pleasure out of losing money, especially money which may be needed to feed my family."

As I said, you couldn't help but like Mr. Merrill. He treated students as if they were somebodies. And it didn't hurt that a lot of girls thought he was the most gorgeous middle-aged male at Tech.

Herman, my strait-laced new roommate, was in the class. He caught up with me on the way out. "Gambling is a curse," he said. "I had an uncle who lost his paycheck at a race track four weeks in a row. His kids actually went hungry until my dad found out about it and took them some food."

I shot back, "Commercial gambling is a service to those who choose to bet. Your uncle didn't have to bet his paychecks."

"Bull!" Herman snorted. "Race tracks and casinos prey on weak people. They're leeches, that's what they are."

I pulled back my fist. "You callin' me a leech?"

"Yeah, if you ever run a damnable casino."

Howie waded through the crowd that had gathered around us. "Stop it, you two! You're roommates."

Herman and I never discussed the subject again. I knew better. Herman was bigger than I was.

And I never brought casino gambling up again in a class.

Chapter 16

"A Drifting Skiff"

Saturday, September 29. Herman was getting dressed for the freshman reception in the lounge of the big women's dorm, Caraway Hall. "You goin', Hefley?" he asked.

"Sure, I'm still a freshman, ain't I?"

"When are you going to stop saying ain't?" Herman scolded.

"When you stop lecturing me about my chosen profession."

I clipped on a ratty-looking bow tie that allowed me to squeak by the dress code, threw on a green coat bought from Blackjack winnings, and grinned at ole straight-laced Herm. "Let's go."

The faculty and administration were there in force when we arrived. Mr. Merrill and Mr. DuLaney were discussing the San Francisco conference of the United Nations. Coach Tucker and Mr. Tommy were talking about Tech's prospects for the upcoming football season.

"We're gonna win the conference," Ole Ephod Tucker predicted. "I feel it in my bones. I know it from watching my boys in practice."

Herman spotted a girl he wanted to meet. Unfortunately for him, she was cornered by three vets. "Best I could get was a 'hello, glad to meetcha,'" he reported back.

The stag line of boys waiting for a dance wound half way around the lounge.

Jeri Lynn and Marie were helping serve punch. I edged over and plucked a punch cup from Marie's dainty hand.

"If you run out of boy friends," I kidded, "then I'm available."

I moseyed over to one of the card tables set up along the side of the lounge. Nobody wanted to get caught playing for money. I strolled back for more punch and some of the little bitty sandwiches with no tops or crusts. Howie and a couple of vets were making small talk with Jeri Lynn.

A big hand caught my arm. Whitey, the Baptist Student Union guy. "We've got a cookout coming up at Reverend Goodbar's house. Monday night at seven. I'll get you a ride."

When I didn't answer, Whitey whispered in my ear, "Remember, Jesus loves you."

I surprised myself by saying, "I know that."

"Then you'll come to the cookout."

"Nope. I ain't no Baptist."

Sunday, as usual, I slept late, got up at ll:30 and drifted over to the dining hall. Students were supposed to dress for Sunday dinner, but I never had. Georgie, wearing a snazzy blue sports coat and matching tie, waved me over to his table. He could hardly wait to tell me, "I'm a Wonder Boy. I made the team as a tackle."

"The first team?" I posed, thinking this was impossible.

"No, the second team. Coach will play me if Jerry Stovall gets hurt."

Cheers resounded from a table near the front door of the eatery. "Yeah, Coach! Go get em, Coach!"

Ole Ephod and his wife were coming in to eat. The cheers were spontaneous. First one table, then another. "Rah! Rah! Rah, rah, rah! Wonder Boys! Tucker! Wonder Boys! Tucker!"

Swiveling his head from one side to another, Coach waved at the cheering students and faculty. He'd been waiting since 1942 for this kind of heady response. That was when the Arkansas Intercollegiate Athletic Conference had stopped play to support the war effort.

Forty-eight hopefuls had reported for the pre-season 1945 practice, including my pals, Georgie and Howie. Fifteen were war veterans. Only Cobb Fowler, who had played on the Tech team in 1940, had any previous college football experience. The student paper called him "The Ding Dong Daddy From Dumas (his hometown)."

Coach scheduled a warm-up game against the Bacon Indians, a non-conference opponent from Muskogee, Oklahoma. Even with the seats wet from a soaking, morning rain, the bleachers were packed. I had never seen a real football game before. Having two pals on the squad, I was at Buerkle Field with bells on, taking a seat on the first row of the steel

bleachers. I was directly behind the Wonder Boys'
bench and facing the Wonder Peppers' cheerleaders
cavorting on the track between the bleachers and the
bench.

Mr. Marvin Williamson raised his baton and
struck up the band. The players, clad in traditional
green and gold uniforms, came swooping from their
dressing room underneath the stands. The crowd
jumped to their feet and yelled. We sang along as the
band struck up the standard song of southern colleges
in that era, "Oh, I wish I were in the land of cotton...
Look away, look away, look away, Dixie Land." Joe
Sidney and the black housekeeping employees of
Tech sang along without any evident embarrassment.

The Tech cheerleaders began prancing on the
track before the bleachers.

> Yea, Arkansas, Yea Tech!
> Let's go team! Let's go!
> Yea, Green! Yea, Gold!
> Go, Team! Go Team!
> Go, Go, Go!

After winning the coin toss, Bacon chose to
receive on the wet field. Bacon's receiver ran Tech's
kick back to their 27 where after a short gain they
were forced to punt. Cobb Fowler, Jack Willis and
Carroll Trimble took the pigskin to the Bacon 2
where Fowler plunged over for the first TD. Willis'
kick was good and Tech led 7 to O.

After that the game was a rout.

Late in the fourth quarter, a chorus of girls began
hollering, "We want Georgie! Give us Georgie!"

Coach must have heard them for he slapped
Georgie on the back and shoved him onto the field.

Cobb scored again. Bacon's receiver took the Tech kickoff and ran straight toward Georgie. Ole Georgie leaped and brought the runner down to earth. The ball was loose! A green uniformed player grabbed it up for an interception. Cobb took the ball across the goal stripe on the next play.

Final score, 80-0.

After the game I waited around for Georgie outside the dressing room. He emerged wearing a big possum grin. "How'd I do, Blackjack? How'd I do?"

"Super," I told him. "You're the wonder of the Wonder Boys."

Georgie punched me playfully in the ribs. "For that, you and I are gonna go ridin' around town tonight. Maybe we'll see a movie at the Ritz."

We saw Ole Blue Eyes Sinatra and Gene Kelly play two sailors on shore leave who got involved with a pretty singer. Nothing risque, but very romantic. All around us, couples from Tech were cuddling. Georgie sighed. "'Fesser, I wish I had a girl. They like to ride in my convertible, but they don't want to go single with me. I've asked a bunch and they all turned me down. Now with all the vets, I'm afraid I don't have a chance."

I sought to give him encouragement. "You're a football player now. Girls love football players. Why don't you ask Emma?"

"She turned me down before. You think she'd go on a date with me now?"

"Won't hurt to try."

Seeing the movie made me homesick for Rosemary. I wrote Daddy to meet me at Lurton on the following Saturday. I skipped my Saturday classes to catch Uncle George Sutton's Red Ball bus.

Daddy and Monk were there right on time.

Daddy stopped only once to shoot a squirrel on the way back to Judy. When he parked in front of the store my four sisters came running out, with Louise carrying little Johnny. Mama trotted right behind them, her arms outstretched.

Mama, as usual, had a raft of questions, mostly about my new roommate and my grades. "Herman," I told her, "is stricter than you, and I haven't been in class long enough to know how I'm doing."

As soon as I could, I slipped across the street to the Brandts. "Surprise! Surprise!" I squealed.

Rosemary came bouncing out. "Well, if it isn't James Carl. I didn't expect to see you here today."

"Here I am," I announced. "How about us goin' to the picture show tonight?"

Her voice dropped. "Oh, James Carl, Kenneth's home and I said I'd go with him."

"Well, can I go too? Both of us took you before."

She shook her pretty little noggin. "Kenneth agreed to it then. I don't think he would now. But if you'll let me know when you're comin' home again, I'll let you take me. If I'm still here," she added. "Mother and Daddy have been talking about moving back to Illinois where he can get regular work."

After a little more small talk, I went back to the store and checked on my punchboards and slot machine. They were right where Mama had put them when I had left for Tech.

Sunday afternoon, Mama rode with Daddy to

take me back to Lurton. "When will you be back?" she asked. That's when I told her about my two Saturday classes. I saw tears glistening in her eyes when she said, "I'll miss you a whole bunch, but I want you to put your studies first."

The football team had won their second game in a row — against a Louisiana college — while I was at Judy. Georgie gave me a blow-by-blow description. "We only beat 'em 14 to nothing. We'd done better if Coach would have let me play more. Hey, you know what. Emma turned me down, but I got a movie date with a pretty little freshman from Clarksville named Julie. She's better lookin' than Emma anyway."

I had to say it. "That's what comes from being a football star."

"Yeah, I reckon so," Georgie agreed, without recognizing that I was stretching the truth. He wasn't really a star — yet.

The next game pitted Tech against a conference foe, the Henderson State Teachers' Reddies from Arkadelphia. Tech's Wonder Boys easily outclassed the Reddies, who never threatened. The final score was 22-0. The only bad part was that Georgie got a sprained ankle and had to be helped off the field. All the next week, Georgie hobbled around on crutches, extracting sympathy from anyone who would give it. Come Saturday, though, he helped Tech beat the Ouachita Baptist Tigers, also from Arkadelphia, 31-0. Georgie played most of the second half and did so well that he was hard to pal around with for a while.

His big gripe was that Julie Doolittle had turned him down for a second date. "How could she do that to me, a big football player?" he moaned aloud to me. I let him have it. "Probably because all you did was talk about yourself." His only reply was a grunt.

Tech's biggest opponent had always been Arkansas State Teachers College at Conway. The campus rocked with cheers and anticipation. Georgie ran wind sprints every day to show Coach that his ankle was fit.

Teachers won the toss and elected to receive. Tech's Carl Sorrels intercepted a pass and raced to the 15. Jack Willis picked up a yard, then Cobb Fowler passed to J.C. Bohannan for the TD.

Tech led 26-0 at the half. Teachers was never in the game. The one-sided tussle ended 65-0.

On his way to breakfast Monday morning, Georgie stumbled on the dining hall steps and broke a bone in his right ankle. Coach pronounced him out for the season.

Georgie was heartbroken. His parents were coming for the big Dad's Day celebration on Thanksgiving when Tech would be pitted against Ouachita Baptist College again. "Because of my injury," he moaned, "Mother and Dad won't be able to see me play."

Herman's folks were also coming to the big wing-ding, which hadn't been held during the war years. Herman encouraged me to invite my parents. I laughed. "Mama won't close the store, even if it is a holiday. Daddy wouldn't wear a necktie if they paid him. And he wouldn't know a football from a pig's toe."

"Why don't you ask them?" Herman challenged. "They might come."

"There'll be other fathers here without neckties," Herman said. "Your folks will have a good time."

Still, I didn't invite them, and was glad I didn't when I saw the program. Mama would have had to bring my year-old baby brother, John Paul. He would have started crying during the formal speeches and fancy choir music. There wasn't a country song on the program. I could just see Daddy squirming while the choir warbled "O Beautious Heavenly Light."

The football game was another piece of cake. Tech pounded Ouachita 26-0. Georgie even got to impress his parents a little when the announcer in the press box called his name along with the other team members.

I didn't tell anyone that my mid-semester grades were my worst yet. An F in chemistry, Ds in Latin, Algebra, and Botany. My best mark was a C in Economics.

I skipped my two Saturday classes again and took the Red Ball to Lurton. Daddy was there waiting as I had requested in a letter. "Yer Mama hain't very happy with yer grades that come in the mail yesterday," he said.

Mama gave me a smile and a hug when I walked in the store. She teared up when I said, "Mama, I'm sorry my grades weren't any better."

Mama didn't raise her voice. "James Carl, you learned fast when you were a little boy. You could read when you were three years old and you graduated from high school at 13. I so hoped that you would enter medicine, and when you chose business, I thought that was all right. Now we get a report card with one F, three Ds, and only one C. You must not be spending much time studying. Whatever do you do with your time?"

The door, mercifully, squeaked open bringing Uncle Will Smith, the aging Justice of the Peace. Mama turned to fill Uncle Will's grocery order, taking me off the hook. I didn't let myself be alone with Mama for the rest of the time I was home.

Back at Tech I was lost in the subjunctive in Latin —I didn't understand the subjunctive in English, so how could I possibly learn it in Latin? In algebra I was mired in quadratic equations. In chemistry Mr. Mac was beating my brains out with benzene molecules and nitric acid. In botany I was buried in horsetails and club mosses. Economics wasn't quite as bad. I had no trouble following Mr. Merrill on the principles of supply and demand.

Football and Blackjack were my major diversions. Tech won every game of the first post-war season, and was scored on only once in the second face-off against the Henderson Reddies. Georgie had an answer for that. "If I'd been out there, the Reddies wouldn't have made that touchdown."

Cobb Fowler brought Tech national fame by being the top scorer of the nation in state college football. The bad news was that Cobb had played out his eligibility, since he had performed for Tech before the war. The good news, Coach Tucker said, was: "We've got a Navy vet named Zig Thigpen coming next season who may be another Cobb."

"Won't matter to me," I told Georgie. "I'm not gonna be here."

"You're not dropping out again? 'Fesser, you'll never get through college this way."

"Georgie, I don't need college to run a gambling business."

During recent months drinking on campus had gotten real bad. The vets drank in their rooms and even in the lounge. They didn't like to be told where they couldn't drink and when they had to be in the dorm at night.

The gambling increased with the drinking. I sat at a table in the lounge and waited until the other guys got soused. Then I'd lay my big bets and clean up.

From early morning until late at night, I laid bets. Out of the dorm early for breakfast, I swaggered in front of the dining hall taunting guys to pitch half dollars at cracks in the sidewalk. After class, I sashayed down to the gym and bet on basketball goals shot from the free throw line. After supper, I headed for the Wilson Hall lounge, soliciting players for a card game.

One evening past midnight in early December, I was dealing Blackjack to a bunch of bleary-eyed guys in the lounge. Our money lay on the table.

"Ahem! Ahem!"

Everything stopped. All eyes turned toward an open pane in the door leading into Mr. C.W.C. Aulsbury's apartment. Mr. C.W.C. was fish-eying us and writing on a pad.

"Pick up your cards," he ordered, "and go to your

rooms. I'm turning in your names to Coach Tucker."

Coach John "Ephod" Tucker, also the dean of men, called a meeting of the Tech male students in the lounge. I got there before he did and slouched down behind a high-backed chair so ole Ephod couldn't see me from the front.

The crowded room fell dead quiet when Ephod stalked in. He didn't start with a prayer, as student meetings did, but waded right into his subject.

"The drinking and gambling has gotten out of hand," he announced.

He began calling the names of the "gamblers" Mr. Aulsbury had given him. I was last on the list.

His eyes roved across the room. "Hefley? Blackjack? Where are you, boy?"

I raised my hand. "Here, Coach."

"Stand up and look at me!"

I slowly stood. "Here, Coach."

He glared at me, anger reddening his eyes. "My name is not 'Here.' Address me as 'Sir.' "

"Yes, sir."

"Hefley, you are the worst influence on our campus. If you don't shape up, we're going to ship you back to Mount Judy. Understand?"

"Yeah."

He raised his voice. "DIDN'T YOU HEAR ME? SAY, 'YES, SIR.' "

"Yes, sir," I squeaked back.

"LOUDER!"

"YES, SIR!"

"Now about the drinking…"

"Sir," I pleaded, "I don't drink."

"I didn't say you did. You're way under age, anyhow."

He called the names of several vets, adding, "You men are old enough to know the rules on campus. When we say, 'No alcohol permitted,' we mean just that." His acid gaze swept the room. "Understand?"

Heads bobbed all around.

I went home for the two-weeks' holiday break. Daddy picked me up at Lurton on Saturday and we rolled into Judy just before two p.m. The street was full of people, farm wagons and old jalopies. I pulled my punchboards and slot machine from Mama's hiding place, plopped them on the counter and opened for business. By five o'clock I'd taken in 13 dollars, not an unlucky number, I presumed. By closing time, around seven, I was 15 dollars and 75 cents richer than when I left Tech.

The semester had two more weeks to run after I got back to the campus. I snoozed through chemistry, algebra, Latin and botany. Now and then I woke up in economics.

Herman laid down the law about Blackjack games in our room. Red wouldn't make his room available, saying, "The Lord has taken away any desire I ever had for gambling." After Coach Tucker's tirade, I didn't dare start a game in the lounge.

When a new movie came to town, I begged Georgie to give me a ride. When Georgie had better things to do, I walked.

Among other flicks, I saw "Keeper of the Flame" with Spencer Tracy and Katharine Hepburn; "The

Keys of the Kingdom," starring Gregory Peck; and "Something to Shout About," a happy little musical featuring Jack Oakie and Janet Blair. All good entertainment that helped pass the time until the semester was over.

I guess Mr. McEver, on the last day of chemistry, summed me up pretty well: "'Fesser, you are a drifting little skiff rolling in the waves. God only knows where you will come ashore."

I packed my suitcase and headed home. My semester grades followed a week later: one F, three Ds, and a lone C in economics. Same as at mid-semester.

There was no congratulatory letter from the dean. No, "We look forward to having you with us for the spring semester."

Twenty-two months before I'd arrived at Tech and been acclaimed a boy wonder. Good professors had sought and failed to set my boat on course.

Chapter 17

"Closed by Sheriff Burdine"

Back in Judy, I pulled out my punchboards and slot machine and reopened my gambling business. One afternoon I happened to spy on a shelf a letter to Mama from Hazel Brandt. Curious, I opened it without asking Mama's permission. Rosemary's mother said they were moving back to Judy. Then she added in a kind of postscript: "I'm praying that James Carl will get saved." I laughed out loud.

I was glad to see Rosemary back. She was a year older and very sassy. In my culture, females didn't talk back to males. This one did, saying I had become a "smart aleck." I called her a nasty name and ran out of her house. Mrs. Brandt broke up the next squabble and declared us too young for dating. It didn't matter. A few months later the Brandts moved to Houston.

My gambling trade tapered off again. The picture show man stopped coming to Judy on Saturday night. With the increase of cars and trucks, more people were driving to Harrison and buying goods there. Fortunately, for us, Daddy's coon dog business was making money.

Much of my time was spent lounging lazily on our store porch, waiting for a customer to show up, dreaming of having my own casino. I was there one afternoon with my two most frequent companions, Billy Wayne Hume and O.J. George, when an old sedan creaked to a stop before us.

Two twenty-something young women stepped out and, in crisp Yankee accents, introduced themselves as Florence Handyside and Helen Lievie, new missionaries from Hasty. "We want to hold young people's meetings in the school on Monday evenings," said Helen, the dark-haired one. "Do you fellows know who we should talk to about getting permission?"

I directed her to the chairman of the school board, Uncle Bill Hefley, who was snoozing on the post office porch. The Yankee women returned shortly and announced that Uncle Bill "said it's okay for us to use the school. You fellows come and invite all your friends. We'll play games and sing and have some interesting Bible stories."

I winked at my pals and promised, "We'll be there."

The three of us had a fun time several Monday nights, scuffling, jerking chairs from under other boys, dropping bugs under girls' collars. When Florence, the blonde, started the music with her accordion, we sang off key. When she launched into a Bible story, we giggled and laughed at inappropriate times.

I had made Coach Tucker angry with my impertinence. Not even with help from Billy Wayne and O.J. could I make Florence and Helen mad.

When we created a disturbance they'd say, "Fellows, please behave," and, "Could you wait until the close of the meeting to do that?"

They came in good weather and bad, driving 15 miles along a dirt road and through two creeks. "Once, the water ran through the floorboard of our car," I heard Florence say. "The car drowned out, but the Lord helped us get it started again."

Florence was from New York, Helen from Pennsylvania. They had gotten to know one another at the Moody Bible Institute where both were foreign missions majors. "Our mission boards," Florence said, "require some practical home experience before sending us overseas."

I guess we were that "experience."

In the spring of 1946, they began a study of the life of Christ. Florence glowed as she talked about her Savior. "Can you imagine the God who created the universe becoming like one of us? A servant? A sacrifice for our sins? Can you imagine?"

I listened quietly for a change, pondering the implications of this. If I'd been asked, I would have probably said I believed in God. But I was far from being on speaking terms with Him. I certainly had no desire to affiliate with any church.

Florence seemed to be talking directly to me. "You think you're too good or too smart to believe? The real problem may be that you're just too chicken to look and see if Jesus is who He claimed to be."

For a moment, I explored the possibility of accepting Christ as God in flesh and the sacrifice for my sins. If I did acknowledge Him, I wondered, *What church should I join? Uncle Bill Hefley's Church of Christ? Uncle Dan Hefley's happy Pentecostal religion? Aunt Lucy's Jehovah Witness dogmas? The Baptist faith of Reverend Goodbar, Whitey, and my former gambling buddy, Red at Tech? Or the Methodist denomination which President Hull and many of the Tech faculty embraced?*

Florence seemed to be reading my mind. "Are you thinking, 'What church should I join? Whose doctrines should I accept?' Don't jump ahead too much. Start with Jesus. Ask God to show you if Jesus is real. Listen to what the Bible says about Him."

Sparks of rebellion fired into flame: *I'm better than many church people. I know guys at Tech who drink and gamble on Saturday night and catch the church bus on Sunday morning. I don't drink or smoke or chase bad girls, like these fellows. Maybe I gamble, but I play fair.* So I reasoned.

"Forget about other people?" I heard Florence say. "Don't always be comparing yourself with someone else. If you hide behind a hypocrite, you're smaller than he is. We're just beginning our study of the Life of Christ. As we proceed, keep asking, 'What is Jesus saying to me? What does He want me to do?' "

Week by week, Florence and Helen carried us through the life of Jesus of Nazareth, from Old Testament prophecies of his coming to his New Testament birth, ministry, death, resurrection and promised return. Slowly I conceded that Jesus might be the Son of God. If he wasn't, then he was a first class lunatic. But how could a crazy person perform miracles and speak such marvelous words?

Florence and Helen's last night came. As on previous Monday evenings, they closed with a song, during which they invited young people to "accept Jesus as Savior and come and stand at the front of the room with us."

No one had ever responded. Now at the close of their last meeting at Judy, Florence held out her arms as Helen started the song.

>Softly and tenderly Jesus is calling,
>Calling for you and for me.

"Come and trust in Jesus," Florence implored. "Won't you come tonight?"

Nobody moved. I steeled myself. *I'm not going to fall for this. One religion is as good as another. I don't have to be religious to go to heaven. If there is a heaven.*

I heard Florence say, "Bow your heads as we close in prayer."

I felt relieved. I had stood my ground again.

Florence and Helen moved from Hasty to Lurton, where, Hazel Brandt told me later, they lived in a one-room shack with cracks so big that snow blew onto their beds in winter. Subsequently, they became foreign missionaries in Asia. So Hazel said, for I never saw them again.

May arrived in full bloom. C.B. Hudson and Junior Johnson, my high school classmates at Judy, would be graduating from Tech. The three of us had enrolled at the same time, two years and two months before. Marie, Emma, Red, Whitey, Howie, Jeri Lynn and the incomparable Georgie would also receive their junior college diplomas. If I had hadn't dropped out a couple of terms and hadn't flunked two required subjects, I would be marching through the Armory with them. Now I was only a dropout, a kid with a little gambling business in a poky little town, a horseshoe pitcher, a hillbilly fisherman.

Many of our relatives were moving to other states, Missouri, Oklahoma, Kansas, and California. Mama and daddy would not be leaving. They had income from the store and Daddy's traffic in coon hounds. My eye was on Nevada. But what casino would want to hire a skinny 16-year-old college flunky?

"No big deal," I told myself. "I'll save my money and wait 'till I'm 18. Then I'll be off to Vegas or Reno." I visualized myself as I had seen gamblers in picture shows. Rolling up to a fancy hotel in a limo. Doffing my black hat to beautiful women. Raking in a stack of chips at a Blackjack table.

To this point, I had spent most of my gambling winnings on clothes and fishing gear. I began thinking about opening a bank account when an ex-Marine dropped $40 on my punchboards and slot machine one Saturday afternoon in the fall.

The loser was Troy Tennison, a distant cousin who lived about a mile west of Judy. His mother blew a gasket when he told her about losing the money. She drove straight to the county seat at Jasper and unloaded on Sheriff Russell Burdine.

"Ain't commercial gambling again' the law in Newton County?"

Sheriff Burdine, who had gained a big reputation for closing down moonshine stills, allowed that gambling as a business was illegal.

"Then why do you let Fred Hefley's boy run a

gambling business in their store at Judy?"

"Aw, James Carl jist makes a few nickels and dimes off little punchboards," the lawman, a good friend of my family, said. "Other stores have punchboards too. If I tried to stop ever'body bettin' on somethin', I wouldn't have time for anything else."

"Russell, you've been too busy catching moonshiners to know whut's goin' on at Judy. James Carl took $40 from my boy. Did you know that he also has a slot machine?"

Russell's eyebrows raised. "No, I didn't know that. I'll take care of your problem," he assured Troy's mama.

Russell sent a message to my folks, saying, "I'm comin' over tomorrow to check on a complaint that James Carl is running a gambling business in your store."

Mama came to me all upset. She was afraid we might be fined, or I might even be put in jail.

"Don't worry," I told Mama. "I'll hide my boards and the slot machine where he can't find them."

I shoved the stuff into a niche behind the counter, and stuffed wrapping paper around the punchboards and slot machine. I avoided Sheriff Russell by going fishing the next day.

The sheriff strolled into the store around one o'clock and bought a soda pop. Daddy was off somewhere with his hound dogs. Russell sipped his drink and chatted with Mama about this and that. Finally, he asked about me.

"Oh, he's gone fishin'," Mama said.

"Well, when he comes home you tell him I've had

a complaint about his little gambling enterprise. If I hear anuther'un, I mout' have to take somebody to jail."

"Sure," Mama said, "I'll tell him. He's a good boy."

"I know he is. I just don't want to hear that he's runnin' punchboards and a slot machine again."

Mama gave me the message when I got home. "Son," she said, "I don't see any harm in your punchboards and slot machine. But Russell says they're against the law and we have to obey the law."

The tree leaves were dying and fishing had turned poor. The Brandts had moved to Texas. Florence and Helen no longer came. Daddy was looking forward to the winter coon hunting season. I didn't care all that much about spending three and four nights a week in the woods. And I was still much too young to catch a bus or hitchhike to Nevada and get a job in a casino.

The worst times came after the kids went to school in the morning. I had nothing to do but sit around all day, with only the old men to talk to. I listened to radio soap operas in the afternoon, but after awhile I got sick of "Oxydol's Own Ma Perkins," "Helen Trent," "Just Plain Bill" and "Our Gal Sunday." If it hadn't been for the radio newscasts, the weekly newspaper and more exciting evening dramas such as "Inner Sanctum" and "Gangbusters," I think I would have died from boredom.

I listened to the conclusion of the Nuremberg war crimes trials. Herman Goering, second in command to Adolph Hitler, was among those sentenced to death. Before he was scheduled to be hanged, Goering took a fatal dose of poison.

Across the blue Pacific, Emperor Hirohito of Japan announced a new anti-war constitution. Never again, the Japanese leadership vowed, would they lead the nation into international conflict.

War and violence continued elsewhere. Zionist terrorists blew up the King David Hotel in Jerusalem. French warplanes bombed Haiphong, killing some 6,000 Vietnamese, launching their vain effort to hold onto colonial Indo-China.

Five new students from Judy were now enrolled at Tech. Two were kin. Eileen Holt, a second cousin, had been my first playmate. James Carl Hefley, son of postmaster Lloyd Hefley, Daddy's first cousin, had been a fishing buddy. Though our names were the same, everybody in Judy knew our identities. He was "Gander," Lloyd and Dora's boy, and I was "'Fesser," the oldest of Fred and Hester's large brood.

Coming home for weekend visits, they caught the Red Ball to Lurton as I had, where they were picked up and taken down Highway 123 to Judy. I asked them about faculty: "Is Mr. DuLaney still twirling his watch chain and teaching Arkansas History? Does Mr. Merrill still sit with his big legs crossed behind his desk and talk about social problems? Are Mr. Tommy and Miss Lela Jane Bryan still making eyes at each other? Is Miss Massie still handing out Ds and Fs in English?" The answer to all my questions was "Yes. Nothing has changed since you were there, except there are a lot more students."

I read about the Tech football games in the

weekly Harrison paper that Cousin Noel, the North mailman, brought every Thursday. It didn't matter that the news was a week late.

Ole Ephod's boys won the state conference for the second year in a row. The big star this season was fullback Zig Thigpen, the vet from Russellville, who was named all-conference and a second string All-American. "You oughta see that Zig run," Gander said. "Some say he's as good as Cobb Fowler."

One day in late November, Mama, little Johnny and I were the only people in the store. "It's gettin' cold," Mama complained. "Go bring in some wood."

I brought in three sticks from the woodpile beside the store and stoked up the fire. My brother Monk and my four sisters would not be home from school for two more long hours.

Mama passed me a little book that looked familiar. It was a Tech catalog. The more I read the more interesting it became. "Mama," I said wistfully, "do you suppose Tech would take me back if I promised to make better grades?"

Mama grinned. "Why don't you write and ask them?"

That very evening I wrote a letter to Dean Turrentine, apologizing for gambling and goofing off in my studies, saying that I'd like to come back to Tech, if the college would accept me.

Within a week Dean Turrentine wrote that I would be welcomed back. He enclosed an application form.

Chapter 18

"'Fesser, the Preacher"

Sunday, January 26, 1947. Nearly three years from the time I first registered at Tech as a crawdad catching, marble shooting, 13 year old.

Once again, Daddy drove me to Lurton to catch the Red Ball to Russellville and Tech. A big timber truck pulled in for gas while I was waiting for Uncle George Sutton's bus. The truck was loaded with staves, bound for a distillery where the staves would be used for making barrels to preserve alcohol.

A lean, sweaty fellow with honey-brown hair and bullet eyes climbed out of the cab. I'd seen his picture in the Harrison paper, but couldn't place him.

He greeted the store owners, Irving and Ruby Sutton, and asked for a Coke. Irving glanced at Daddy and me. "Zig hauls staves for his daddy when he isn't in class at Tech. He may be a big football star down there, but he's jist an ole country boy up here."

"Zig Thigpen!" I almost shouted. "You're the Tech fullback that made all them touchdowns last fall. I read about you in the Harrison paper." I extended my hand. "My name's James Carl Hefley.

This here's my daddy, Fred Hefley. He brought me here to catch the Red Ball back to Tech."

I didn't tell Zig that I had been laying out a whole year. The Red Ball was running late. Zig sipped his Coke and we talked about some of the Tech teachers, including Miss Massie. I confessed that I had flunked English under her.

About that time Uncle George Sutton walked in and said hello to everybody. He noticed that I had on a dress shirt and pants and said knowingly, "So you're going back to Tech. Wa'l, git yer suitcase and I'll take you to Russellville."

Uncle George dropped me in front of Wilson Hall. I left my suitcase in the lounge and walked over to Ole Main to get my room assignment. Registration would not come until the next day.

A new secretary was in charge of handing out the keys. "Wilson and Rock dorms are full," she said. "Since you've been out a year, we'll have to put you in the old barracks behind the barn on Red Hill. There are only 60 boys assigned out there. You'll have a room by yourself."

I'd been past the barracks that had been used to house extra military personnel during the war. "It's way out in the weeds," I protested.

The secretary eyed me with amusement. All she said was, "You're a country boy," and handed me the key.

I walked back to the Wilson lounge, picked up my suitcase, and lugged it a half mile to the old barracks. The key wouldn't turn the lock. I finally had to force the door open. To the right of the door stood a scarred, wooden dresser. A large footlocker, labeled **U.S. Army Surplus**, took up space near a narrow single bed. Behind the bed was a cavernous closet choked with spider webs. Fortunately the room came with a broom. I cleared out the cobwebs, hung up my clothes, and washed in a dingy bathroom down the hall. By then it was time for supper.

Ole Main was jammed with students registering the next morning. Room and board had gone up to $30 a month. "Inflation," Dean Turrentine's secretary explained.

Mr. Weedin was my advisor again. He frowned as he ran his pencil over my record. "You failed English 113A once and only made a D the second time. Think you can pass 113B?"

"Only if I don't have Miss Massie," I allowed. "I couldn't pass her in an airplane."

The dark-haired business prof grimaced. "I'll put you under Mr. T.J. Cole. He's a new teacher. What are your career plans?" he asked.

"To manage a business." Since he didn't bring it up, I decided not to mention my casino ambitions.

"Okay, I'll sign you up for Business Management. And you should have accounting, psychology and sociology. You'll need them all in managing a business."

He raised his eyes to mine. "James, if you have any problems, come and see me. What's past is past. I want you to succeed in the future."

I took his extended hand. "Mr. Weedin, I'm going to try. I really am."

On my way to the business office, I passed Miss Massie. This time she recognized me instantly.

"Why, Mr. Hefley, you're back. Congratulations." That was all she said as she walked away.

I had six subjects, all heavies, more than I had taken previously. Amazingly, I liked the teacher of every one.

Dr. Orby Southard, one of only three Ph.D.s on the faculty, piqued my interest in psychology. Pipe in one hand, book in the other, he said, "You want to know why people behave as they do? Study psychology." Actually, I learned more about myself than anyone else. For one thing, I had let all the bragging about my smartness go to my head. My big-headedness led me to think that I knew what was best for me in all circumstances.

Mr. T.J. Cole, the new English professor, motivated me to take a crash study in grammar. I even quit saying ain't. "Ole King Cole," as many students called him, proved to be a delightful soul, especially to the girls who thought he looked like Cary Grant.

Mr. Roy Weedin showed me how to create a successful business. "First," he said, "decide on objectives. What do you want your business to produce? Where do you want it to be five, ten, twenty years from now?"

Mr. Weedin also taught accounting, which he said "tells you your assets and liabilities and gives you a base for planning ahead."

Mr. Merrill, a gentle giant and my second most-favorite person (next to Mr. Tommy) on campus, whetted my desire to know more about economics and sociology.

My classes turned out to be so interesting and rewarding that after a couple of weeks, I told myself,

"'Fesser, ole boy, you're beginning to learn a few things."

Six heavy courses didn't give me much time to think about gambling. I spent a good deal of time in the library, which I'd never done before. I chatted with professors without nursing a chip on my shoulder. I even came to greet Miss Massie in a civil way. "Mr. Hefley," she said one day in the library, "I think you're beginning to grow up."

I still held to the ambition of running a casino in Nevada. I wanted to prove myself before people. I dreamed of driving back to Judy and Tech in a new Cadillac, wearing a $300 suit and sporting diamond cuff links and a jeweled stickpin.

I still didn't attend any of the dances. The girls I knew were gone. With my studies I didn't have time.

Engineers Day rolled around again, featuring the usual formal dance, and initiation rights. I was in the library studying and didn't hear about the craziness until the next morning at breakfast. Agri Day was more of the same.

I joined the Business Club. Mr. Weedin saw that the meetings were conducted with dignity. Among the other clubs, only the Baptist Student Union invited me to their get-togethers. I certainly wasn't prime social material.

I never went to a BSU event. I never attended a church in Russellville. I did think a lot about what the missionaries, Florence and Helen had said.

My mind ran back and forth: *What if I do make a fortune in the gambling business? Is that all there is to life? What if there is a heaven and hell? What if the Bible is really true? What if Jesus Christ really is God?*

I remembered a verse from the Gospel of John quoted by Florence: "I am the way, the truth and the life; no man comes to the Father but by me."

What about Muhammad, Buddha, and other founders of great world religions? Was Jesus truly the only way to heaven? Was Jesus a deluded drifter? Or was he really God?

While kicking such alternatives back and forth in my mind, I went home for the six-day spring break, beginning Thursday, April 3. I should have been feeling good. Mama kept bragging on my mid-semester grade card which she'd received in the mail, two Bs, three Cs and only one D, in accounting. By far the best grades I'd made since entering Tech.

There really wasn't much to do in Judy. I was afraid to pull out my punchboards and slot machine. The fishing season wouldn't open until May 15. I could talk to the bench warmers, read, listen to the radio or pitch horseshoes. Nothing very exciting on my agenda.

In horseshoes we were pitching singles with the winner staying up until he lost. I had a dead eye and could average three ringers out of every four pitches. Saturday evening, I had just won my 12th game in a row, when Mama walked up and touched my shoulder. "Son, a Preacher Denny has come to hold church in our front room. Please come in and hear him." she implored.

"But what about the Grand Ole Opry, Mama? The radio's in the front room."

"You can listen to the Opry after the preacher leaves."

"Aw, Mama," I said grudgingly. "I'm still winning horseshoe games."

The old "hotel" where we were living was the only house in Judy with an upstairs. Mama kept beds there and also behind a partition in the store. We kids could sleep wherever we wanted. I usually slept upstairs in the hotel when home from college.

Mama pleaded and wheedled until I finally agreed to come and hear the preacher who had driven into town and asked around until Mama told him he could preach in our house. I never asked Mama his denomination. I just didn't care all that much.

The singing had already started when I slipped through the front door and climbed to near the top of the dark stairs.

From my perch, I saw a bespectacled, little half-bald man sitting near the door and singing heartily. I figured he must be Preacher Denny.

The singing stopped. The preacher stood up and introduced himself as a Baptist mountain missionary. He told a joke about one of Daddy's hound dogs which got Daddy's attention. He made some friendly remarks about other people he had met in Judy, cousins and uncles of mine. I began to relax.

Then he opened a big, black book. "Now let's see what God's Word says about all of us."

His sermon was plain, pithy and somewhat painful.

"The Bible says that 'all have sinned and come short of the glory of God.' That's a double-l all. You.

Me. Everybody on God's earth.

"The Bible says our hearts 'are deceitful and desperately wicked.' Your heart. My heart. Everybody's heart.

"The Bible says, 'It is appointed unto man once to die and after that the judgment.' That means you. Me. Everybody. Nobody's excluded."

He slapped his big Bible for emphasis. "Thank God, there's a way of escape. Jesus died on the cross for my sins, for your sins. You just tell him you're a sinner. Claim his forgiveness. Tell him, 'Yes, Lord. I accept.'"

He wasn't saying anything I hadn't heard from Florence and Helen. As with them, I began making excuses.

I don't need this forgiveness. I don't drink, cuss, smoke, tell dirty stories, or chase girls.

But I'm greedy, selfish. I like to take money from people. He's telling the truth. I am a sinner. I do need God's forgiveness.

The preacher announced a song familiar from Florence and Helen's meetings. "Everybody, please stand and sing," he requested.

> Just as I am without one plea,
> But that Thy blood was shed for me,
> And that Thou bidst me come to Thee,
> O Lamb of God, I come, I come...

He stood with extended arms. "Come and take my hand and say you'll accept Jesus as your Savior tonight. Come now, come."

My heart was pounding, my palms sweating. Something within me said "yes." I stumbled down the stairs, a skinny, 16-year-old college sophomore.

Preacher Denny came rushing to meet me.

"Do you believe? Do you accept Jesus?" he asked.

"Yes! I believe. I believe that Jesus died for me."

"What's your name, son?"

"James Carl Hefley." I pointed to Daddy. "I'm Fred Hefley's son. The coon hunter. It was his dog that you told a joke about."

The preacher lifted his voice so everyone could hear. "Praise God, Fred Hefley's boy is trusting in Jesus!"

Mama and Daddy were both crying. I couldn't remember ever seeing my Daddy shed a tear.

After a few more stanzas of "Just as I Am," Preacher Denny gave a prayer of dismissal. Then he counseled briefly with me. "Read the New Testament, son. Start in the Gospel of John. Learn all you can about Jesus. I'll be back and see you in a few days."

After Preacher Denny left, I went upstairs and fell into a deep, sweet sleep. Upon arising the next morning, I found a tattered old Bible and began to read. After awhile, I heard Mama calling. "James Carl, your breakfast is getting cold."

I dressed and hustled downstairs. Everybody else had eaten and gone. Even Mama had left for the store, but before leaving she had filled my plate with biscuits, eggs, and flour gravy.

When I returned to Tech, I hit the books hard. Sunday came and I thought of going to church. But which one? The town churches on Main Street had always looked so huge, cold and foreboding. I doodled around the room until it was too late to walk over to the campus and catch one of the buses.

Sunday evening I walked to town by myself and took in a brainless movie at the Ritz. Boring. Back in my room, I found the Bible much more interesting.

I went home the next weekend, hoping to see Preacher Denny. I was still in bed Sunday morning when he came clumping up the stairs, calling, "James Carl? Are you awake?"

We talked a few minutes, then he prayed. Raising his head, he surveyed me with a smile. "Boy, I think the Lord may be calling you to be a preacher."

"I think so, too." The words just popped out of my mouth without any premeditation.

"We're starting a Sunday school," he said, "beginning a week from tomorrow in the Brandt's old house. How about you giving a devotional?"

I had never heard the word "devotional."

"Just pick a Scripture and talk on it for about five minutes. You can do it," he said.

I had always been able to talk in front of people. I came home that weekend and delivered the goods. "Brother Otis," as he had instructed me to call him, was ecstatic. "How about preaching at the Deer Baptist Church next Sunday. Just take several scriptures and talk a little on each one. Don't try to imitate me or any other preacher. Just be yourself."

Mama and Daddy drove me there, taking along Monk, my four sisters, and three-year-old John Paul. Blind Ernie Cheatham, one of the deacons, pronounced my sermon, "one of the best I've heard."

For the rest of the semester, I took classes during

the week and came home to preach or give the devotional at the Judy Baptist mission in the old cobble-stoned house where Rosemary and her parents had once lived.

The graduation exercises at Tech came on May 25 in the Armory, a day before the final exams were to begin. That meant I had to be on campus when 126 sophomores received their junior college diploma. With my sorry academic record, I lacked at least one, and possibly two more semesters to qualify for a diploma.

The academic procession formed in front of Ole Main. Led by President Hull and the graduation speaker, Judge J.H. Carmichel from Little Rock, the line moved toward the Armory. I stood on the sidewalk and watched the procession go by.

Mr. Tomlison, who had recently been ill was in the line, grinning and waving at onlookers. I spotted Dean Turrentine, Mr. Hardin, Mr. Merrill, Mr. Cole, Mr. Rollow and a beaming Miss Massie among the dignitaries as they passed by me.

Was it just my imagination or did Miss Massie wink at me?

Could it be that she'd heard of my improved grades? Did she know my vocational aspirations had changed?

A familiar voice sounded from across the street. "Hey, Blackjack. It's me — Georgie."

Ole Carrot-top himself. I hadn't seen him for a long time. A beautiful blonde clutched his arm as I walked back to meet them.

"My bride, Amanda, Blackjack. We got hitched

four days ago and are on our honeymoon."

I shook Amanda's bejeweled hand. Then I asked Georgie, "What are you doin' back? Didn't you get your diploma last year?"

"Yeah, but I heard that Tech may become a four-year college. I wanna be one of the first to sign up for my degree. Where's your cap and gown?"

"I still lack some courses. But I'm doing better. Make Bs in Business Management and Economics and a C in English."

A look of amazement crossed his face. "What happened? You quit gambling?"

"Yes," I replied. "God has changed my life. I've even busted up my slot machine and cut up my punchboards."

"Aw, you're puttin' me on."

"Nope. I'll be preachin' next Sunday at the First Baptist Church of Jasper."

Georgie surveyed my serious face in puzzlement. Then he broke into a broad grin. "Well, I guess miracles never cease. Instead of callin' you 'Fesser or Blackjack next they'll be callin' you Preacher!"

"Afterword"

Has it been over 50 years since I first stepped into Dean Turrentine's office? It has and I am back at dear old Arkansas Tech University which now has more faculty than there were students when I first enrolled.

On this warm Thursday afternoon I have no trouble finding the revered residence where President Hull once lived. I never set foot in the dwelling while at Tech. "Welcome to Alumni House," Alumni Director Sharon Mullins bubbles as I enter. She points to a table and chairs. "We already have a place set up for you to do your interviews."

"First," I say, "I'm gonna take a sentimental journey around the campus."

I stroll across to Buerkle Field and peer through the webbed steel fence. There is the spot where I tackled Georgie in Phys Ed.

I cross the street to what I think must be Ole Main. I replay the sights and sounds of March 10, 1944. Later I learn that Ole Main was torn down and a white-columned replica was erected on the site.

On to Wilson Hall which looks just the same. Bailey Hall is gone. Off to the east I see the huge gleaming mound that is the John E. Tucker Coliseum.

The Red Barn is no more. The School of Liberal and Fine Arts now bejewels those grounds.

The old gym building is in place, but the Techionery sign is gone. I peer through a window and see crates where the jukebox once stood.

I walk east to the Tomlinson Library, Mr. Tommy's namesake. Peeking in, I see a flock of young researchers perched before computers.

After another half hour of looking into new buildings named for Tucker, McEver and other revered faculty from the 1940s, I end up back at Alumni House. There I spend the rest of the afternoon and the next day visiting with old grads living in the Russellville area. They bring me up to date on my old professors.

"Miss Massie was in her 70s before she finally married," Heartsill Bartlett, class of 1937, notes. "She and her husband moved to California where she died.

"Mr. Tommy and Miss Lela Jane Bryan dated off and on for 15 years. They died without ever tying the knot."

Firmon "Nig" Bynum, a revered football alumnus, may have been the last person to see Mr. Tommy alive. "One evening I gave him a ride home. We set out in my car and talked until around ten o'clock before he finally said, 'I'd better get on in the house.' He was discovered in a chair the next morning, dead.

Nig also shares memories of his close friend and coach, John "Ephod" Tucker. "The loss of his first wife in the 1950s devastated him for a while. He married again, only to lose that wife to death. The third time he married a widow and died himself not long afterward."

One by one I'm told that all of my old professors

have passed on. All except Mr. Rollow, who is legally blind. Sharon says he lives close by the campus and a phone call from her brings him tap, tap, tapping through the front door. I rise and introduce myself as one of his former "D" students.

We sit and talk about old times. Mostly I ask questions, such as:

"What did you hope to get across to your students?"

"That education is important if they ever want to be somebody."

Our conversation runs over an hour. I stand and place a hand on his shoulder. I pray out loud, thanking God for my dear old professor.

I walk him to the door. "I can make it the rest of the way," he declares.

A month later I'm back for Homecoming. The big day starts for us old codgers with a Gold Club Breakfast at the Holiday Inn. A train of old alums give testimonies about the "good old days." Tucker is canonized. Merrill, DuLaney, Weedin, Rollow and Mr. Tommy are lauded. Even Miss Massie comes in for praise.

Except for the football game, the big event for the day is the Homecoming Luncheon. We sing the alma mater. President Bob Brown speaks briefly about "the great ones of the past." The Tech cheerleaders bounce up to lead us in cheers. "Gimme a T, gimme an E, gimme a C, gimme an H. Tech! Tech! Tech!"

Outside, the band is marching, the drums are booming, the football players are warming up. Some of the players are black.

The cheerleaders are activating the bleacher-packed crowd. The homecoming queen is crowned. A green and gold caped and masked figure comes racing down the track in front of the stands. He crashes through a paper sheet. Behind him gallop the Wonder Boys.

The coin is tossed. The Boll Weevils of the University of Arkansas at Monticello elect to receive. "Defense! Defense!" chant the cheerleaders.

The Boll Weevils score first. Tech takes the ball and marches downfield for a TD. The kick is good. The score is tied 7-7.

A hand touches my shoulder. Bert Mullens, father of Sharon, points to a stylishly dressed woman in black, seated a few rows up in the stands. "Coach Tucker's widow, Vicki."

I elbow my way upward and introduce myself as writing a book about my time at Tech in the 40s. "Your late husband was then both football coach and dean of men. He knew me well, but I wasn't one of his favorite students."

Above the noisy hoopla of the homecoming game, she recalls the circumstances of Coach Tucker's death in March, 1982. "That Sunday morning I found him dead in our bed. The doctor said if he had lived, he would have been a crippled man. He'd had a massive heart attack.

"John was a very modest man," she recalled. "He didn't think they were going to name the Coliseum after him. I said, 'Of course they will.' He was very thrilled when they did."

"Thank you for sharing this," I say. "I'll let you

get on with the ball game."

Tech makes a 38-yard field goal, putting the Wonder Boys ahead of the Boll Weevils. I recognize a man with a video camera. Jack Hamm, Dean of Tech's School of Systems Science. Jack is the first graduate of Mt. Judy High School to earn a Ph.D.

"My dad, Elmer Hamm," he notes, "played football at Tech and later taught here for several years. I came here on a basketball scholarship in 1959."

"How did you get into science?"

In answering he recalls an episode with Miss Massie. "I'd been away on a basketball trip and came in to tell her I wasn't prepared for her upcoming exam. She said, 'Son, sit down here and let me help you get your act together a little bit.' She had me make out a study schedule for all my courses. 'Get organized. Get yourself together,' she said. I followed that schedule religiously. It made a great difference in my ability to do college work and later to teach."

The game is ending. The cheerleaders, students and returning alums are counting down.

"Tech-nine-eight-seven-six-five-four-three-two one. Yeah Tech!

"Yeah, Tech!" I echo. "Thank you," I whisper.

Meet the Author

James Carl "'Fesser" Hefley graduated from Mt. Judea, Arkansas High School at age 13. He was an off-and-on student at Arkansas Polytechnic College from 1944 to 1947. He later received the B.A. and honorary Litt.D. degrees from Ouachita Baptist University, the M.Div. from New Orleans Baptist Theological Seminary and the Ph.D. from the University of Tennessee.

He has served as a pastor, editor, freelance writer and a college lecturer on mass communications. He has written over 70 books, including two with Ozark locales, *Way Back in the Hills* and *Way Back When*.

Dr. Hefley presently lives in Hannibal, Missouri with his wife Marti (an editor and writer), where he is CEO of HANNIBAL BOOKS and the director of the Mark Twain Writers Conference.

James and Marti have three daughters and six grandchildren.

Fessor Goes to College, by James C. Hefley

_____Copies at $5.95=_____

Way Back in the Hills, by James C. Hefley. The ordginal colorful autobiography of the author's growing-up-years in the Ozarks.

_____Copies at $4.99 = _____

Way Back When by James C. Hefley. Relive the "good ol' days" when the first white settlers made their way deep into the Ozark Mtns.

_____Copies at $5.95 = _____

Way Back in the Ozarks, by Howard Jean Hefley & James C. Hefley. Stories of a boy named "Monk," his dog & his coon.

_____Copies at $5.95 = _____

Way Back in the Ozarks, Book 2 by Howard Jean Hefley & James C. Hefley. "Ozark Monk" relives the tale of Danny Boy.

_____Copies at $5.95 _____

Way Back in the Ozarks, VHS VIDEO TAPE Meet "Ozark Monk" as he entertains you with stories from his first book. Filmed on location.

_____Copies at $15.95 _____

Please add $2.00 postage and handling for first book, plus $.50 for each additional book.

Shipping & Handling _____

MO residents add sales tax _____

TOTAL ENCLOSED _____

Name _____

Address _____

City_____ State____Zip_____

Mail coupon with check or money order to: HANNIBAL BOOKS, 921 Center St., Hannibal, MO 63401 Call 800-747-0738 for credit card orders. Satisfaction guaranteed.